Cookery terms explained

For Granny White, who suffered from Parkinson's for twenty-seven years and Grandpa who lovingly nursed her.

For Bill Snell, without his kind interest this book would never have been.

Cookery terms explained

BY VANESSA TIMMIS

WESTON PUBLISHING

Cookery terms explained

First edition 2001

ISBN 0 - 9530130 - 2 - 2

Copyright © Vanessa Timmis, Weston Publishing Limited

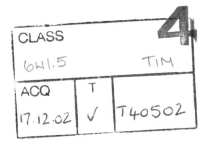

Designed and illustrated by John Miles

Printed and bound in the UK
by Butler & Tanner, Frome and London

Foreword

Cookery terms explained is exactly what it says, all the basic terms used in cookery defined in a helpful and concise manner with just the right amount of information.

It is an extremely useful book for beginners through to new professionals, and the clear organisation into chapters and sections, with a comprehensive index, makes it easy to find any term quickly.

Basically this little pocket-sized book is essential for anyone interested in cooking and the language of cooking, and personally, I do love the drawings.

Soyez sage. Eric

ERIC TREUILLE
Books for Cooks

Contents

Author's note

Fresh out of catering college and eager to prove myself in the big wide world, armed with everything I thought I needed to know (ha ha), I started my first job as assistant cook (actually a glorified washer-upper) twenty years ago. Rapidly I found out that what I had learnt was only the tip of the iceberg, but I managed to bluff my way through various jobs in Europe, the States and Australia, soaking up information on the way like blotting paper. On my return several years later, friends and relations seemed to be under the impression that my phone number was a culinary hotline and myself the resident Agony Aunt. How misguided they were!

'What on earth is a bain-marie?'

'How do you clarify butter and why should I bother?'

'What is the equivalent of an American or Australian cup in ounces or grams?'

Gradually the idea of gathering all this information into a book started to take root. Many months of stalking fruit and veg vendors, annoying book shop assistants and loitering in libraries finally led to this book.

So sit back and relax, help is at hand!

Acknowledgements

The author gives thanks to the following:

My parents for all their unquestioning support in whatever I have done and wherever I have been.

Terry for giving me deadlines, it could have taken another ten years otherwise!

Delia (Roughley, not Smith!) for being an inspiration since we left college twenty years ago.

Last but not least, Tim, who is the best thing since sliced rye bread!

The publisher wishes to thank the following for their contributions to this book.

Nessie for writing the book, John Miles for the book design, illustrations and jacket design, Eric Treuille for writing the Foreword and Trevor Howe for the photograph of the author.

Further thanks are due to the following for their advice and/or support, Fiona Watson, Eric Treuille at Books for Cooks, Della Alim, Sofie Sutherland, Colleen Farr, Ruth Harris, Peter Towse, Louise Miles, Adrienne Maguire and Nicky Grimbly at agm marketing, Doug Badenoch at Butler and Tanner, and Kirstie Kemp and Bill Norris at Central Books.

General cookery terms

General terms

Additive   A substance added to foods as a preservative or to enhance the colour, taste or smell.

Agar-agar   Widely used in Oriental cookery, this gelatine made from seaweed is a tasteless white powder that will keep a dish firm without refrigeration, and is suitable for vegetarian use.

Al dente   A term used to describe the way food is cooked to a chewy or firm consistency, still with a bite but not overcooked.

Arrowroot   The edible starch of a South American plant made by grinding the roots and stems into a fine white powder which is used as a thickening agent. Arrowroot contains no gluten and may be used instead of cornflour.

Aspic jelly Traditionally made from clarified stock but can be bought in the form of crystals. Aspic jelly is colourless and is used to decorate savoury buffet dishes such as cooked salmon or for pouring into raised pies.

Au bleu   A culinary term applied to freshly caught fish boiled in salt water, seasoned with vegetables, herbs, and white wine or vinegar.

Au four   A term for any food cooked in the oven.

Au gras   The French term for meat dressed with a rich gravy or sauce.

Au gratin   A term applied to certain dishes coated in a sauce topped with breadcrumbs or cheese and baked brown in the oven or under a grill.

Baking powder A raising agent for cakes, scones, etc. made from two parts cream of tartar (acid) to one part bicarbonate of soda (alkali). Care must be taken to keep the powder dry as contact with moisture will set the chemicals working.

Baking soda An alternative name for sodium bicarbonate. This will work on its own as a raising agent if the recipe contains an acid such as buttermilk, soured milk or cream of tartar.

Ballotine Poultry or meat boned, rolled or shaped, and cooked. It may be served hot or cold.

Barbecue Outdoor cooking, usually over glowing charcoal, giving the food being cooked a delicious, slightly smoky flavour. It is also the name for the apparatus on which the cooking is done.

Batter A mix made from flour, eggs, milk/water/cream and sometimes beer. Sweet batters for pancakes and waffles contain sugar while savoury batters, such as Yorkshire pudding batter, do not.

Bean curd See *tofu*.

Beurre manie A mixture of equal parts of flour and butter that has been kneaded together to form a paste. It is used to thicken sauces, stews, etc. towards the end of cooking.

Bicarbonate of soda Alternative name for sodium bicarbonate, also known as baking soda.

Biscuit A small flat crisp cake which may be sweet or savoury. Taken from the French *bis cuit*, meaning twice cooked. In earlier years, sailors lived off biscuits, which had been pre-baked before boarding to keep them from going mouldy and re-baked when required. Today they are only cooked once and are at their best when freshly baked.

Blancmange A British pudding, despite its French name, made from milk, sugar, flavourings and gelatine, set in a special mould.

Blanquette A stew made from white meats enriched with a sauce thickened with cream and egg yolk.

Bouchée A small round piece of toast or pastry, the size of a mouthful, topped with a filling.

Bouquet garni The name used for a small bunch of herbs tied together which is used to flavour stews, soups, etc. Usually bay, thyme and

> HANDY HINT
>
> **Keeping biscuits crisp**
> Place two sugar lumps in the container.

3

parsley are used, although other herbs such as marjoram or tarragon may be added.

Bread The staple diet in many parts of the world, and different recipes can be found in every country. Generally wheat flour is the most commonly found flour in commercially made bread, but other cereals such as rye are also used.

Brochette French word for skewer, and also used to describe food cooked on a skewer.

Brûlée French term meaning burnt or caramellised. It usually describes a dish with a crisp topping of caramellised sugar, for example, crème brûlée.

Brunoise French term for any food cut into small dice or cubes, most commonly vegetables.

Bun Small loaves of yeasted bread, generally sweet and sometimes with the addition of dried fruit. Also used for small cakes baked in bun tins.

Burger Round and fairly flat patty of ground beef and seasonings which is fried or grilled and usually served in a bun with relish.

Butter Churned pasteurised cream is used to make delicious butter. Salt may be added to enhance the flavour and this also acts as a preservative. The colour and flavour of butter is determined by the breed of cows from which the milk is taken, their diet, the time of year, the salt content and the way in which it is made.

Butterscotch A hard, brittle confectionery made with butter, sugar and water or a soft sauce made from butter, sugar and cream.

Cake Baked or fried mixture of flour, fat, eggs and sugar. A raising agent and flavourings are also added.

Canapé Served with drinks, this small appetiser usually consists of a round of bread or pastry with a flavoursome topping.

Caramel Heated or chemically treated sugar used as a brown colouring, a flavouring in desserts, or a confectionery that tastes rather like a soft toffee.

Carbohydrate An energy-giving substance, containing carbon, hydrogen and oxygen, eg. sugars and starches. Foods containing a high level of carbohydrates include bread, cakes, biscuits, pasta, cereals, flour and sugar.

HANDY HINT

Cake mixture splitting
Add a little of the measured flour to bring the mixture back.

Casserole   Food cooked and served in a dish. A selection of vegetables, meat or poultry with water is cooked in a container with a tight-fitting lid to minimise evaporation.

Celsius   A scale for measuring temperature on which the freezing point of water is 0°C and the boiling point is 100°C. The scale is also known as Centigrade.

Chantilly   Whipped cream that has been flavoured with sugar and vanilla.

Chapelux   Browned breadcrumbs.

Cheese   Cheese is made from the curds of soured milk or milk that has been coagulated with the help of rennet, a curdling substance obtained from the stomach of unweaned calves, or if vegetarian cheese, from artichokes. It can also be made from whey, the thin liquid left over from cheese-making.

Chocolate   A rich sweet confection made from cocoa butter derived from cocoa beans from the cacao or cocoa tree.

Chowder   A thick North American soup, traditionally containing shellfish.

Citric acid   A weak acid found in citrus fruits, raspberries and other fruits. It is used for making lemonade and boiled sweets on a commercial scale.

Cochineal   The dried and ground bodies of a certain beetle from Mexico make up this dark red food colouring, most commonly used for colouring icing pink.

Coffee   A drink made from roasted and ground beans from the evergreen trees of the Coffea genus.

Compote   A mixture of fruit stewed in sugar syrup and served either hot or cold.

Confectionery Sweets, candies and chocolates considered as a group.

Confit   Salted and sometimes spiced pieces of meat, usually duck and goose, which have been preserved in fat.

5

Conserve	Whole fruit jam.
Consistency	The word used to describe the density of a mixture.
Consommé	Clear soup made from either meat, game, poultry, fish or vegetable stock.
Cookie	The Scottish word for a plain bun or the North American word for a biscuit.
Coulis	A thick purée of fruit or vegetables.
Court bouillon	The French for fish stock which is used for poaching fish or as the base of a fish sauce.
Crackling	Scored pork skin that is crisped up during roasting.
Cream	Cream is the larger lighter fat particles that rise to the surface of whole cow's milk, and has a much higher butterfat content than milk.
Cream of tartar	A main ingredient in baking powder, this fine white powder is crystallised from tartaric acid, found in grapes.
Crêpe	French term for pancake.
Croquette	A mixture of meat, fish or vegetables together with mashed potatoes, formed into a cylindrical roll, coated with egg and breadcrumbs and deep-fried.
Croûte	A shaped piece of bread deep-fried or toasted, traditionally served with game dishes.
Croûtons	Deep-fried or baked small pieces of bread which are served with soup or salad.
Crudités	Raw vegetables cut into batons or sticks and served with dips, usually as an appetiser.
Curd	The solid part of soured milk, which has been separated from the liquid whey.
Curdle	Describes what happens when fresh milk or a sauce separates into solid and liquid through over-heating or by adding acid. The term also applies to cake mixtures that have separated when eggs have been added too rapidly to creamed butter and sugar.
Custard	A sauce made from egg yolks, sugar and milk. It can be bought commercially as a powder to which milk is added.
Dessert	A popular British name for a sweet course served at the end of a meal.

Dip　　A flavoured thick sauce, which can be scooped up for eating by, for example, raw vegetables, crackers or bread.

Dough　　A mix made from flour and liquid, sometimes with added fat and/or sugar and/or yeast.

Dripping　　The fat which has melted off the roast joint during cooking. Commercially bought dripping is white in colour and has been strained.

Dropping consistency When a food mixture, for example, cake mixture, is thick enough to fall off a spoon in one dollop, rather than running off as a liquid.

Dry goods　　Commercial term for groceries that do not need refrigeration.

Dumpling　　A small dough ball made from flour, water and fat and cooked in soups, stock or stews.

Eggs　　Most commonly the reproductive body laid by the domestic hen. They are used in many different ways. The raw yolk will emulsify with oil or melted butter to create mayonnaise and hollandaise. The whites, beaten to a firm consistency and with added sugar, make meringues. The whole egg will thicken hot mixtures like soups, stews and sauces by coagulating in the heat and holding the liquid in suspension. Food that is dipped into beaten egg will keep the coating of breadcrumbs in place while being deep-fried, and stop the food from absorbing oil and becoming greasy. They are, of course, delicious on their own, whether poached, boiled, fried, in omelettes or scrambled. The eggs of other birds are eaten, for example, goose eggs. Duck eggs are extremely rich and are best used in custards and mousses. Gull's eggs are only available in early spring, and tiny quail's eggs are delicious hard-boiled and served with celery salt.

Emulsion　　An even dispersion of one liquid within another, for example, in mayonnaise or hollandaise.

En croûte　　A French term used to describe meat or fish wrapped in pastry and then baked.

> HANDY HINT
>
> **Test eggs for freshness**
> Put in a bowl of water. If they sink they are fresh, if they float they are bad.

En papillote A term used to describe food that has been cooked in an envelope of greaseproof paper, tin foil or pastry.

Enzyme Protein produced by a living organism which acts as a natural catalyst in a specific biochemical reaction. Enzymes allow, for example, the digestion of food as it passes through the gut.

Escalope A thin slice of meat cut from the fillet.

Extract Concentrated flavouring extracted from certain foods.

Farce See *stuffing*.

Farenheit A scale for measuring temperature at which the freezing point of water is 32°F and the boiling point 212°F.

Fat Energy-giving food made up of carbon, hydrogen and oxygen. Vegetable fats are derived from plants and animal fats are derived from animals. Fats can be stored by the body after digestion.

Fermentation A chemical reaction in which the action of an enzyme breaks down an organic compound. This can be seen from the foaming when sugar is added to yeast.

Fillet A prime, lean and expensive cut of meat from the loin area, or the flesh from the body of a fish with the bones removed.

Fines herbes French phrase for finely-chopped, fresh or dried mixed herbs.

Fish Cold-blooded animals that live in water with backbones surrounded by edible flesh. They usually have fins and are covered in scales. They are an excellent source of protein.

Flambé A dish soused in warmed alcohol and then set alight before serving at the table.

Flan Open tart filled with a sweet or savoury mixture.

Flapjack A thick biscuit made from oats, butter, sugar and syrup, baked in the oven and cut up into pieces while still warm.

Fleurons Small, crescent-shaped puff pastry garnishes.

Fondue The Swiss are famous for fondues, for example, melted cheese or chocolate. Small pieces of appropriate food are speared on a fork, dipped into the molten mixture and eaten. Fondue bourguignonne is meat cooked in hot oil, and fondue chinoise is meat cooked in hot stock.

Fool   A cold dessert of puréed fruit folded into whipped cream or custard.

Forcemeat   See *stuffing*.

Freeze   Preserving food by storing at a temperature of minus 18°C or 0°F.

Fricassée   White stew of chicken, rabbit or veal that is thickened at the end of cooking with cream and egg yolks.

Fritter   Food that has been coated in a batter made with the addition of stiffly beaten egg whites and deep-fried for a light, crisp texture.

Frosting   North American term for icing.

Fruit   An edible part of a plant that is all or part of the seed-bearing part of the plant, for example, raspberry, apricot, plum.

Fudge   A delicious confectionery made from boiled sugar, milk, butter and flavourings.

Fumet   Intensely-flavoured liquor, usually reduced fish stock.

Galantine   Poultry or meat that has been boned, sometimes stuffed, rolled, cooked, pressed and glazed. The dish is always served cold.

Game   A general term used for particular birds and other animals that are are hunted by sportsmen at set times of the year, depending on the animal.

Garnish   Decorative trimmings used to ornament savoury and sweet dishes.

Gateau   French word for a rich cake.

Gelatine   A substance made by boiling parts of an animal carcass, usually feet or trotters, head and legs. Gelatine is available commercially as powder, granules and leaves and is used to thicken or set sweet and savoury dishes.

Gigot   Whole leg of lamb.

Gill   Liquid equivalent to $1/4$ pint/150 millilitres.

Glace   French for ice cream.

Glacé   Refers to substances preserved in sugar with a shiny surface, for example, glacé fruits, glacé cherries.

Gluten	A constituent of wheat and other cereals, which is stretched by steam and air during baking and supports the body of a cake or bread.
Goulash	A Hungarian stew or soup made with the addition of paprika.
Gravy	A sauce made from the pan juices of a roast and stock, and usually slightly thickened with flour or cornflour.
Griddle	A thick iron plate which is heated up until very hot and used to cook griddle cakes and scones.
Herb	An aromatic plant used to enhance the flavour of sweet or savoury dishes. Usually it is the leaves that are used.
Hors d'oeuvre	Mouth-sized pieces of food served as an appetiser. It is also used as another word for starter.
Ice cream	A mixture made from a base of custard or cream, sugar and eggs, which is then frozen.
Icing	A sweet covering or filling for cakes or patisserie made from, for example, icing sugar and water for royal icing, or butter, flavourings and icing sugar for butter icing.
Jardinière	French term for a garnish of young spring vegetables.
Julienne	French term for vegetables cut into strips the same size as a matchstick.
Junket	A traditional British dessert made from warm sweetened milk, brandy or sherry. It is thickened by the addition of rennet.
Jus	Meat, fruit or vegetable juice.
Jus lié	Thickened gravy.
Kebab	Cubes of marinated meat, traditionally lamb, skewered and grilled. The dish originated in the Eastern Mediterranean. Other foods such as fish and/or vegetables may be made into kebabs.
Kosher	Food prepared according to orthodox Jewish laws.
Lactic acid	Naturally occurring acid found in milk, cream and some butters when they have turned sour.
Lard	Soft white pig's fat which is very high in saturated fatty acids.
Leaven	An agent, such as yeast, used to raise dough.

Legume	Edible pod or seed of a plant, such as a pea or bean, which is eaten as a vegetable. When dried, legume seeds are called pulses.
Liaison	An ingredient or combination of ingredients used for thickening, for example, soups, sauces and stews.
Lukewarm	Blood temperature.
Macaroon	These round biscuits are made from lightly beaten egg whites, almonds and sugar, baked and decorated with an almond on top.
Macedoine	Diced mixed vegetables or fruit.
Margarine	A manufactured fat made from a combination of animal and/or vegetable fats and/or oils. These may include palm oil, coconut oil, cottonseed oil, groundnut oil, whale oil, sunflower oil and soya derivatives.
Marinade	A liquid usually containing an acid, such as vinegar, wine or cider, herbs, onions or spices for flavouring and oil to add richness, which is used to flavour food prior to cooking.
Meat	Flesh that is made up mainly of muscle tissue with some fat. The most commonly eaten meats in this country are beef (cow), lamb (lamb), pork (pig) and veal (calf).
Medallion	French term for food that is cut into a round or an oval.
Meringue	A sweet that is made from stiffly beaten egg whites and sugar which is slowly baked in a cool oven and served with cream when cold.
Meunière	Literally means 'miller's wife', a buttery sauce especially good served with sole.
Mignon	The thin end of beef fillet.
Milk	The liquid food produced by a lactating mammal for her young. Milk contains most of the nutrients required by the human body, including calcium, protein, vitamins and minerals. Most commercially bought milk is obtained from the cow, but it can also be from goats, sheep and water buffaloes.
Mimosa	Sieved hard-boiled egg yolks used as a garnish.
Mincemeat	A traditional British mix of apples, currants, raisins, sultanas, beef suet, port, sugar, almonds, spices and

grated rinds from citrus fruit. Traditionally served at Christmas in individual pies with brandy butter.

Mirepoix   Slowly cooked diced root vegetables and chopped bacon, seasoned with herbs.

Mocca   A blend of chocolate and coffee.

Monosodium glutamate   A powder made from sugar beet pulp, gluten from wheat and Japanese seaweed, which itself has little flavour but enhances the flavour of protein and other foods.

Mousse   A light sweet or savoury dish made from a sweet or savoury base with the addition of eggs, cream and gelatine.

Nibbed   Term for finely-chopped nuts.

Noisette   French word for hazelnut, also used to describe anything nut-shaped or nut-coloured.

Noodle   Generic term for a variety of flat pasta strips of varying widths and lengths, some of which may contain egg.

Nut   A fruit with an edible kernel and a hard outer shell, for example, walnuts, Brazil nuts.

Oil   In the context of cooking, a vegetable or animal fat which is liquid at room temperature.

Omelette   A mixture of beaten eggs, seasoning and a little water is quickly fried in an omelette or frying pan, then folded over. The omelette may contain a savoury or sweet filling.

Oyster   Small piece of meat, the size of a ten pence piece, found on either side of the backbone of a chicken under the leg.

Paella   A traditional Spanish dish consisting of short-grain rice, vegetables, chicken and shellfish. The golden-yellow colour is achieved by adding saffron.

Panada   A roux of fat and flour which makes a white sauce that is twice the thickness of a coating sauce. It is used, for example, as a base for soufflés or croquettes.

Pancake   Made from a pouring batter, these flat, thin cakes are cooked in a frying pan and may contain sweet or savoury fillings. Traditionally they are eaten with lemon juice and sugar on Shrove Tuesday.

Parson's nose The very end tail or rump portion of a bird such as chicken, turkey, goose or duck. It is sometimes called the pope's nose.

Pasty A meat and vegetable filling wrapped up in a pastry parcel pinched together along the top. Originally eaten by the Cornish tin miners for their lunch.

Paté Made from poultry, liver, meat, fish, game or vegetables cooked into a solid mass. Paté may have a smooth or coarse texture and is served with warm toast or bread.

Paupiette The French word for a particular cut of meat, which is a thin slice. Usually this is rolled around a filling, for example, beef olives. Fish fillets can also be used.

Pectin A substance found naturally in some fruit and vegetables. It is a necessary ingredient for the successful setting of jellies and jams.

Pesto An Italian condiment made from fresh basil, parmesan, olive oil, garlic & pine nuts. Excellent with pasta!

Pie A sweet or savoury filling covered or encased in pastry.

Pilaf/pilau A rice-based dish in which chicken or meat is so well-cooked that it falls apart easily and the juices are absorbed into the rice. In addition spices, nuts, dried fruits, vegetables and sometimes saffron may be included. Some pilafs are made with just vegetables or shellfish.

Pith The white spongy layer found under the rind of citrus fruits.

Pizza An Italian flat open tart made from a yeasted dough topped with various savoury mixtures.

Potage A thick soup.

Poultry Domesticated birds bred for the table, including chicken, turkey, duck and goose. The flesh of chicken and turkey is more digestible and leaner than the darker red meat of beef or lamb.

Praline Whole unblanched almonds set in caramel, sometimes crushed to a powder and used in or to garnish desserts.

Protein Compound of carbon, hydrogen, oxygen and nitrogen, and sometimes sulphur. The proteins in food provide the body with essential nutrients for forming new tissue.

Pudding	A light spongy sweet cake mixture that is either baked or steamed, or a savoury mixture, such as steak and kidney, steamed in a bowl lined with suet crust pastry. Also sometimes used as an alternative name for dessert.
Pulse	Dried seeds of legumes, for example, peas, beans and lentils. These all provide a rich source of protein.
Purée	A thick pulp made from either cooked or raw fruit or vegetables.
Quenelles	Fish, meat or poultry that has been ground to a fine paste which is then moulded into spoon shapes, poached in a liquid and served with a sauce.
Quiche	A sweet or savoury open tart or flan, the most famous being quiche Lorraine made with eggs, cream and bacon.
Réchauffé	Reheated dish.
Refrigerate	Keeping food at a temperature range of between 2°C and 7°C, or 35°F and 45°F. This prevents the growth of harmful bacteria and allows food to be safely stored for a variable period depending on the food.
Rennet/rennin	Gastric juices obtained from the fourth stomach of an unweaned calf (this sounds like the recipe for some kind of witches' concoction!). It is used for making junket and cheese.
Rice paper	Edible paper made from the pith of a small tree of the ivy family. It is used for lining baking trays to prevent food from sticking.
Rillettes	Pounded cooked pork or veal put into small earthenware pots and sealed with pork fat.
Risotto	An Italian savoury rice-based dish.
Rosti	A Swiss potato cake made from cooked grated potatoes, chopped onions and seasonings. These are then shaped into cakes and fried in fat or oil.
Roulade	Derived from the French 'rouler', to roll. Describes any dish where a top layer is spread over a base layer and the whole is rolled up.
Roux	Equal amounts by weight of fat and flour, cooked together to form the base of a sauce.
Salad	A dish of raw leafy green vegetables, often tossed with other ingredients and generally served with a dressing.

Salmis/salmi A game stew.

Salpicon Finely-diced vegetables, meat, game or fish bound together in a sauce and used as a stuffing or filling.

Salsa A spicy sauce of raw or cooked chopped fruit or vegetables used as a condiment.

Salt/sodium chloride Most foods contain natural sodium which is essential for our existence. Commercial salt is obtained either from rock salt, or from the evaporation of natural brine, or from the artificial brine obtained from running water into mines to dissolve the salt.

Sandwich In the eighteenth century, the Earl of Sandwich is said to have ordered his roast supper to be brought to him between two pieces of bread so as not to disrupt his game of cards. Thus was born the sandwich, two slices of bread, often buttered, with a savoury or sweet filling, for example, cheese and pickle, peanut butter and strawberry jam.

Sauce A liquid embellishment accompanying savoury and sweet dishes.

Sausage A long thin manufactured food made from the minced meat of various animals, most commonly pork, either pre-cooked, fresh, cured, air-dried or smoked. In Britain a quantity of cereal is added, whereas in Germany this is forbidden. In Italy the salami is made with raw ingredients, brine-pickled and then smoked. Other ingredients used in sausages include eggs, cream, beer, wine, pig's blood, tripe, breadcrumbs, oatmeal, potato flour, onion, garlic and herbs. The casings are made from the intestines of either pigs or sheep, or may be produced synthetically.

Scone Made from a dough of flour, fat, sugar, salt, raising agent and milk. Traditionally eaten in Britain with clotted cream and jam for afternoon tea.

Seafood Edible marine animals such as fish and shellfish.

Seasoning A mixture of substances used to enhance and accentuate flavours, for example, salt and pepper.

Seed The fertilised ovum of a plant from which a new plant can be grown.

Shellfish This term covers molluscs and crustaceans such as snails, oysters, prawns and crabs.

Sodium bicarbonate See *baking soda*.

Sorbet A frozen dessert made from water, fruit juice, sugar and whipped egg white. It is sometimes served between courses to refresh the palate.

Soufflé Egg yolks are added to a thick sweet or savoury base into which the beaten egg whites are then gently incorporated. The mixture is cooked in a straight-sided dish until it is well risen. It must be eaten immediately as it will sink rapidly as soon as it cools down. The oven door must not be opened during cooking for this reason. A cold soufflé is made, for example, from a fruit purée, gelatine and cream into which stiffly beaten egg whites are folded. This is then chilled.

Soup A liquid dish containing a selection from meat, poultry, fish, game or vegetables, stock, water, milk and seasonings. Soups may be thin or thick, and may have added cream.

Spices Aromatic plants, many of which are grown in tropical countries, yield the aromatic spices from varying parts of the plants. These spices are dried and are available whole or ground, and are used for flavouring sweet and savoury dishes.

Spit A thin metal pointed rod used for rotating food over a heat source, such as a barbecue.

Sponge cake A light, dry cake containing eggs, flour and sugar. Generally no fat is used, although some recipes include butter or margarine.

Spread A food product, such as cheese or chocolate spread, Gentleman's relish or peanut butter, which is smothered over another, such as toast.

Starter A bacterial culture added to milk which changes the lactose into lactic acid adding flavour to milk, butter and cheese. Also an alternative name for the first course of a meal.

Stew A dish where meat and vegetables have been cooked in liquid at a low temperature for a long time. A container with a close-fitting lid is used to minimise evaporation.

Stock	The resulting liquid from cooking bones, vegetables, herbs and seasoning together in water.
Suet	The firm white fat that surrounds lamb or ox kidney. It can be used in sweet puddings, such as jam roly-poly, or savoury dishes, such as steak and kidney pudding.
Sugar	Sugar is a crystalline substance obtained from sugar cane or sugar beet. It is soluble, sweet-tasting and, as it is a carbohydrate, energy-giving.
Syrup	A sweet liquid used for sweetening or poaching fruit, made from boiling dissolved sugar and water until the correct consistency has been reached.
Tannin	A chemical found in tea leaves, with a higher content in green tea than in black tea. The amount present depends on the type of plant, where it is grown, and when the leaves are picked. Tannin slows down the absorption of caffeine into the body.
Tapenade	A thick Provençal paste, made from olives, garlic, olive oil, capers and anchovy fillets, traditionally served with toast as an appetiser.
Tart	Baked open pastry case which may have a sweet or savoury filling.
Tea	The world's most popular drink, made from the leaves of an evergreen tropical bush native to China & India. The tea grows at altitudes upwards of 7,000 feet above sea level, and the higher the altitude, the finer the tea. There are two main types of tea, black and green, produced from different treatments of the leaves after they are picked. Black tea leaves are fermented, whereas green leaves are not.
Tepid	Blood temperature.
Terrine	French word for a paté cooked in a china or earthenware lidded dish, which is also called a terrine.
Textured vegetable protein (TVP)	A manufactured protein food produced mainly from soy beans with trace elements added. It is used as a meat substitute.
Tisane	A herbal infusion or tea made by steeping the herb in boiling water. The resulting liquid may be drunk with beneficial effect, for example, camomile aids sleep.

Toffee   This traditional British confectionery is made from syrup, water, sugar, butter and vinegar.

Tofu   Originally from Japan and China, this soy bean curd is low in calories and high in protein.

Topping   A layer of food added to a prepared dish, for example, breadcrumbs, cheese or cream.

Treacle   A by-product of sugar manufacture, brownish-black in colour and strong in flavour.

Trifle   A dessert traditionally made from sweet sherry-soaked sponge cake, custard and lightly whipped cream. There are many different variations on the theme now and they often include fruit.

Unleavened   Describes a product where no raising agent has been added, for example, unleavened bread.

Vanilla sugar   Vanilla pods are added to sugar in an air-tight container and left for a period of time to infuse.

Vegetable   A plant of which part can be used, raw or cooked, to feed humans and/or other animals.

Vinaigrette dressing   An oil and vinegar dressing with added herbs, spices and seasoning.

Vinegar   Wine, cider or malt is fermented to produce a sharp sour-tasting liquid containing varying quantities of acetic acid. Vinegar is used as a preservative and as a condiment.

Vol-au-vent   Puff pastry cases, with the centre marked out before baking so that the lids can be removed, are baked, filled with a sweet or savoury filling and topped with their own lids.

Whole grain wheat   The complete unprocessed grain of the wheat.

Wholemeal   Describes flour or any other product, for example, wholemeal bread, made from the whole wheat grain.

Yeast   A living organism which can reproduce itself under the right conditions. It is used as a raising agent in doughs, breads and some batters. It is important never to use boiling water when blending the yeast as when it reaches $60^{\circ}C/140^{\circ}F$ the yeast ceases to work.

Yoghurt   Yoghurts are made commercially from low-fat or skimmed milk and are injected with a culture of Lactobacillus acidophilus, Streptococcus thermophilus or Lactobacillus bulgaricus. Some yoghurts, especially fruit-based yoghurts, have also had milk solids, sugar, cream and edible gum or gelatine added. Although only some commercial yoghurts are labelled 'live', all yoghurts are so unless they have been pasteurised.

Zest   The outermost part of the rind of citrus fruit. It is often used as a flavouring.

Ingredients

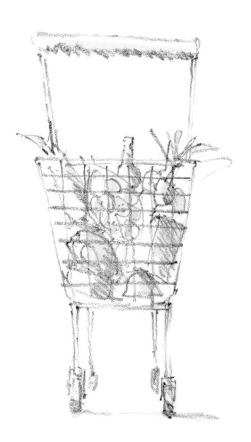

Meat, poultry and game

MEAT

Beef

Meat from bullocks, cows and bulls. A beef carcass should be aged by being hung for at least ten to fourteen days to enhance the flavour and to tenderise the flesh. The lean of good roasting beef should be marbled with fat that melts during cooking to give a moist, tender finish. Minced beef should be red in colour, and if it is pink then there is too high a fat content. The various cuts of beef may be cooked in a number of ways, and some of the most common are listed below.

Roasting Sirloin, rib joints, thick flank and whole fillets.

Pot roasting Flank, brisket, topside, rump and silverside.

Boiling Silverside and brisket.

Salting or pickling Silverside and brisket.

Grilling/frying Suitable for fillet, sirloin, rump, porterhouse and T-bone steaks.

Stewing Suitable for tougher bits of meat such as flank, chuck, clod and shin.

Veal

Meat from dairy calves. The flavour of veal is delicate and tends to be dry unless careful attention is paid to the cooking. It does not have a long shelf life and should be eaten on the day of purchase. The various cuts of veal may be cooked in a number of ways, and some of the most common are listed below.

Roasting Suitable for large joints such as shoulder and loin.

Pot-roasting/braising Shoulder and middle neck.

Boiling/stewing Neck and knuckle.

Grilling/frying Cutlets from the best end of neck and escalopes cut from the fillet are best suited for this method of cooking.

Lamb and mutton Lamb is the meat from a sheep under a year old, older than that and the meat is known as mutton. Mutton needs to be well hung before cooking and, as it has a high proportion of fat, it needs to be well trimmed. The various cuts of lamb may be cooked in a number of ways, and some of the most common are as follows.

Roasting Double or single loin, with the kidney attached, whole leg, shoulder, best end of neck. A crown roast is made from two matching pieces of best end, each containing seven to eight ribs, which are joined together in a circle with the skin side on the inside and the thick ends of the meat at the base.

Pot-roasting/braising Boned breast. Guard of honour is also prepared from two best ends, but the bones are trimmed and cleaned to about two to three inches. The two pieces of meat are then joined and sewn together, skin side up, along the meaty parts of the joints.

Stewing/boiling Breast, middle and scrag.

Grilling/frying Cutlets cut from the best end with a high proportion of bone, chops from the loin and chump chops. A noisette of lamb is a trimmed, round slice from the best end of lamb.

Pork The meat from the pig. It is a prime and tender meat which should be pale pink with firm white fat. As pigs are slaughtered at an early age, all the meat is tender. The various cuts of pork may be cooked in a number of ways, and some of the most common are as follows.

Roasting All pork joints are suitable for roasting on or off the bone.

Boiling Fresh or salted hand, salted leg and salted belly pork.

Grilling/frying All types of chops are suitable.

Bacon, gammon and ham These cured meats from the pig are sold as whole joints or as rashers and steaks which are suitable for grilling, boiling and frying.

HANDY HINT

Crisp crackling on pork
Score the fat with a sharp knife and rub in oil and salt before cooking.

calves liver · Lambs kidney

Offal	Literally means the 'off-fall' or off-cuts from the carcass.
Bath chaps	Smoked cheeks of a pig, usually boiled and eaten cold like ham.
Calves' brains	One of the most popular offal, served with black butter sauce or fried in batter.
Caul	The lace-like membrane around the lower intestines, used for binding sausages.
Chitterlings	Pig's intestines, often used in sausages, which are either fried or grilled.
Feet	Calves' feet and pigs' trotters are high in gelatine and are used to thicken stocks. They can also be boned, stuffed and fried.
Heads	The head from the pig is used mainly in brawn and sausages. The heads from calves and sheep may be boned and stuffed, and served divided into pieces with a sauce.
Hearts	The hearts from calves and lambs are the most tender and are suitable for stuffing. Ox heart is tough and requires long slow roasting.
Kidneys	These should be bought as fresh as possible and be an even mid-brown in colour. Kidneys vary in size, tenderness, strength of flavour and texture depending on whether they are from veal, lamb, pork or beef. They can be grilled or used in stews.
Lights	The lungs, which are not very nutritious, but can be used in stews.
Liver	Beef liver is strong in flavour and quite tough, so is best used for braising and stewing. Pork liver is also strong in flavour and is mainly used in patés. Lamb's liver should be either grilled or fried, and veal's liver, the best in quality, should be sliced thinly and either fried or grilled.

HANDY HINT

Coating meat in seasoned flour
Place seasoned flour in a polythene bag, add meat and shake until all the surfaces are coated.

Marrowbone   A soft substance extracted from the shoulder or thigh bones of oxen or calves after cooking. It is highly nutritious and may be used in sauces and casseroles.

Melt   The spleen of the animal. Pig's spleen sometimes goes in sausages, while the melts from beef and veal may be stuffed, cooked and served.

Sweetbreads   The pancreas gland, located near the stomach, and the thymus gland, located in the throat, of veal and lamb are very similar in taste and are considered a delicacy. Traditionally the glands, one round and one elongated, are sold in pairs and served with black butter.

Tails   The most common is oxtail, which is used in stews and soups.

Testicles   These can be fried in batter, sautéed or cooked in stock and served with vinaigrette.

Tripe   The stomach lining of an animal, most commonly the ox. It is sold bleached and partially cooked, but it still needs further long slow cooking.

POULTRY

Boiling fowl   Can weigh up to seven pounds and are best used in casseroles or stews. These older birds are now hard to find, but can be replaced with a roasting bird.

Capon   A young neutered male chicken which is fattened on corn giving an excellent flavoured meat.

Chicken   Available all year round, fresh or frozen, and usually bought ready to cook. There are many different varieties, for example, the yellow corn-fed chicken is rich in flavour and really tastes of chicken whereas the polythene-wrapped version often lacks any taste and needs a lot of flavouring. This is always reflected in the price.

Duck   Best eaten between six weeks and three months old. Although this bird has less flesh than a chicken, it has excellent flavour and very rich meat.

Goose	The young gosling, up to three months old, is the most tender and ideal for roasting. From eight to nine months the goose becomes fattier and tougher and requires a longer cooking time in a casserole or stew. The meat has a slightly gamey flavour but the goose has very little meat on its bones!
Guinea fowl	Once considered a game bird, now it is bred for the table and as such is considered to be poultry. It may be used for roasting, in casseroles and in any recipe suitable for chicken.
Poularde	As highly regarded as capons, but the female neutered version. The best variety hails from Bresse, in France.
Poulet/spring chicken	Slightly larger than the poussin and cooked in the same way. Allow one bird per two people.
Poussin	Immature chickens without the full flavour of the mature bird. They are best split and marinated, then grilled over a barbecue. Allow one bird per person.
Turkey	This native American bird is best hung for about three days to bring out the gamey flavour. The female hen is more tender than the male and, as the saying goes, the younger the better! It is traditionally served in the UK for Christmas lunch or dinner, accompanied by chestnut stuffing, cranberry sauce, roast potatoes, Brussels sprouts, bread sauce and a clear gravy.

GAME (FEATHERED)

Duck	The most common variety is the mallard. Other types include teal, pochard, scaup, sholver and widgeon. As the duck is very fatty, it is best roasted.
Gamecock	Male game fowl.
Goose	A large bird belonging to the duck family.
Grouse	Considered to be the best flavoured of all the game birds, grouse keeps well and may be roasted or grilled if young. Older birds are best braised or cooked in a casserole.
Guinea fowl	Indigenous to West Africa, this game bird is related to the pheasant and is in season in Britain from late

	spring to early summer. It should be cooked in the same way as chicken.
Hazel hen	A woodland grouse found in Europe.
Hen	A female bird.
Moorfowl	The name given to various game birds including the red grouse.
Partridge	Related to the pheasant, young birds are best roasted, whereas older birds are best suited to casseroling or braising.
Pheasant	This popular game bird is found all over the world and is best when hung and then roasted.
Pigeon	They are best suited for stews or casseroles as these birds are tough.
Plover	These birds are the size of a pigeon and are in season in Britain from August until March. Only the golden and grey varieties are eaten. They are best roasted undrawn and served on a piece of toast.
Quail	Related to the pheasant, and is either roasted, sautéed or grilled.
Snipe	The bird is best roasted whole with its entrails, which are considered to be a delicacy.
Squab	The name given to a four week old pigeon. It is also the North American term given to a small one-portion chicken.
Thrush	This medium-sized brown songbird is regarded as a delicacy in France and Italy.
Widgeon	A small wild duck, often accompanied by an orange and sherry flavoured gravy when roasted.
Woodcock	Related to the snipe, this bird is best roasted or braised with its entrails intact.

HANDY HINT

Mixing or shaping raw minced meat for burgers or meatballs
Wet hands before shaping to prevent meat sticking to the hands.

GAME (FURRED)

Boar Popular in German and Russian cooking, only the meat of the young boar is tender. Older boar need to be hung for two to three days and the flesh marinated before roasting.

Deer There are three main types of deer, red deer, fallow deer and roe deer. Unless very young, the meat of all deer, known as venison, needs to be hung and marinated before cooking. The best meat is taken from the haunch, although the loin and fillets are also very tender. The close-textured, lean and distinctively flavoured flesh may be roasted, braised, stewed or casseroled, and is traditionally accompanied when roasted by gravy, game chips and redcurrant jelly.

Hare The hare belongs to the same family as the rabbit but its meat is more gamey and the flesh is darker. Young hares do not need to be hung and are best roasted, while the older animal is usually hung and the meat used in casseroles, stews and patés. They are in season in Britain from August to March.

Rabbit There is no need to hang rabbit as the flesh is more tender than hare. The flesh may be roasted, fried, stewed, braised or casseroled. A traditional accompaniment to roast rabbit is onion sauce.

Venison See *deer.*

Fish and shellfish

Burbot This round-bodied, lean-fleshed North European fish is related to the cod family. It can be poached, steamed, baked, grilled or fried.

Carp Originally a delicacy in Asia for thousands of years, it can now be found in lakes and ponds worldwide. The medium-oily flesh has a muddy taste and should be scaled, cleaned and soaked in slightly salted water for up to four hours before either baking, frying, steaming or poaching.

Catfish There are many varieties of this fish caught in the northern coastal waters of Europe. The fillets may be baked or fried.

Chub A relative of the carp and usually caught for sport rather than a meal due to the great number of small bones and the muddy flavour of the flesh.

Dace This fish is similar to haddock, only smaller. The flesh is lean with many bones and is best steamed or fried.

Dorado This fish is caught in South American rivers. Dorado is also an alternative name for the seawater dolphin fish.

Eel Available all year round, it can be boiled, grilled or fried, and is particularly good in soups and stews.

Freshwater bream Related to the carp family, bream is not suitable for eating as its flesh is bony and has a muddy taste.

Grayling Similar to trout, and at its best in autumn and early winter after the trout season has finished. The firm white flesh may be poached, steamed, fried, grilled or baked.

Gudgeon Related to the carp family, this small fish is best cooked by dipping in batter or egg and crumbs and deep-frying.

Jackfish   See *pike*.

Loach   Particularly popular in France when fried, this European river fish has a delicious flavour but the flesh is very bony.

Perch   Best eaten from June until December, this oval-bodied fish with its lean flesh and delicate flavour is highly regarded, despite the many bones. It may be fried, baked, grilled, steamed or poached.

Pike   Available from August to February, this round-bodied fish has lean, white bony flesh, and is best poached, steamed, baked, fried or grilled.

Pike-perch   Thus named due to the fact that it resembles a cross between a pike and a perch. The white, delicately flavoured flesh of this fish may be poached, steamed, baked, fried or grilled.

Roach   A member of the carp family, this fish has numerous forked bones. It is usually fried.

Salmon   A fish that spends a large part of its life out at sea, but is usually caught in the lakes of North America and Northern Europe. There are many varieties, the most popular being the pink salmon. It may be poached, grilled or baked, and is also commonly smoked or cured.

Trout   There are many sub-species of this fish, including brown, rainbow, cut-throat, salmon, sea, pink, brook and lake. Related to the salmon family, the flesh is oily and can vary in colour from ivory to deep pink depending on the sub-species and on diet. Ideal for poaching, baking, frying, grilling or steaming.

Whitefish   These fish are similar to herring and can be substituted for trout.

Anchovy
A round-bodied fish, found in warmer waters, growing up to twenty centimetres or eight inches in length, which is readily caught from January to September. Its oily flesh has a very distinctive flavour and may be grilled or fried. It may also be bought preserved in cans, salted, dried, as a paté and as an essence and is an important part of Mediterranean cuisine.

Barracuda
This fish, found in the waters off the Caribbean and the warmer waters of the Atlantic and Pacific, has lean, firm flesh which is often cut into steaks and barbecued.

Bass
Similar in shape to the salmon, the flesh is firm, lean and white which makes it suitable for poaching, baking, grilling, frying or barbecuing.

Blue fish
Caught off the Atlantic coast of America and in the Mediterranean, this fish can be grilled, fried or baked.

Bonito
A member of the tuna family, this fish is found in the Mediterranean, Pacific and Atlantic and is generally sold cut into steaks or salted.

Brill
Found in the shallow waters of the North Atlantic and the Mediterranean, this firm-fleshed flatfish is cooked in the same way as sole, and is best eaten in autumn and winter.

Cod
A cold-water fish, found in the northern areas of the Atlantic and Pacific, which can grow up to ninety pounds or forty kilogrammes in weight. The flesh of the codlings is much firmer and sweeter. The white flesh of the adult fish is lean, easy to digest and usually sold pre-cut due to its size. It is suitable for steaming, poaching, grilling, baking, frying and barbecuing, and is best bought between October and January although it is eaten all year round.

Coley/Boston bluefish/pollack/saithe This fish is caught all year round off the coasts on both sides of the Atlantic. The flesh is lean and darker than cod and it becomes lighter when poached, steamed baked or fried.

Conger eel Caught off the Atlantic coast of Europe and Africa and in the Mediterranean, this eel is best used for soups and stews although it is good stuffed and baked.

Dab This small flatfish is found in North Atlantic waters off the coast of Europe and is sold whole or in fillets. It may be grilled or fried.

Dolphin fish/dorado/lampuga This fish lives in warm waters and is usually bought as fillets or steaks which are grilled, baked or fried.

Flounder A flatfish found all year round in the shallow waters of the North Atlantic. The white flesh is lean and therefore is best steamed or fried.

Garfish/garpike/sea eel A round-bodied fish found in the Mediterranean and the Atlantic off the coast of Europe. It has flesh similar to the oily mackerel which can be fried or grilled.

Greater/lesser weaver Caught in the shallow waters off the coast of Europe, these fish are best used in bouillabaisse but can also be grilled or deep-fried. The poisonous sacs and spines must be removed before cooking.

Grey mullet/striped mullet/black mullet Can be found worldwide, but particularly in the Black Sea. They all have firm well-flavoured flesh and can be stuffed, baked, grilled or fried.

Grouper Commonly found in the Mediterranean, this fish is usually sold in steaks and can be grilled or baked.

Gurnard Found in the Mediterranean and North Atlantic, this bony fish may be poached or steamed and is especially popular in France.

Haddock Caught off Newfoundland and Europe, this fish is often smoked or sold filleted and deep frozen. It can be grilled, fried, poached, steamed or baked.

Hake Related to the cod family, and mainly found off the coast of Ireland, France and Spain. The white, lean flesh is best poached, steamed, baked or fried.

Halibut The largest of the flatfish found in the waters of the North Atlantic and Pacific Oceans. It is mainly sold as steaks or fillets because of its size, and its flavoursome, firm white flesh is best suited to baking, steaming or poaching.

Herring	A small oily fish caught in the North Atlantic and Pacific. The flesh is firm and can be baked, grilled, fried, salted, smoked or pickled. Smoked split herrings are called kippers.
John Dory	A fish caught off the coasts of Europe and Africa, similar to turbot or sole in texture and cooked in the same way.
Ling/tusk	A round-bodied fish related to the cod family and caught in the North Atlantic. It is best poached, steamed, baked or fried.
Mackerel	Caught all year round on both sides of the Atlantic, and in the Mediterranean and Black Sea. The oily flesh is firm and well-flavoured making it suitable for frying, poaching, baking, grilling and sousing. It is also commonly found smoked.
Meagre	This fish is found in the Atlantic and the Mediterranean and is cooked in the same way as bass.
Monkfish/anglerfish	Found in Atlantic and European waters, only the tail is sold. The white flesh is lean and has a texture and flavour similar to lobster. It may be poached, baked, grilled or fried.
Needlefish/skipper/saury	Similar to the garfish but fatter, it can be fried, baked or grilled.
Opah/kingfish/sunfish/moonfish	Available worldwide, this fish has a plump oval body which can be eaten fried. In Japan it is often eaten raw.
Plaice	Found in the shallow waters of Europe, this flatfish can be caught all year round. It has white lean flesh and can be poached, steamed, baked, fried or grilled either whole or in fillets.
Pollack	A North American name for coley.
Red mullet	This fish is best fried, grilled or baked, and is cooked and eaten ungutted.
Red snapper	Found in the waters around the Gulf of Mexico, this small fish can be baked whole or filleted.
Sardine/pilchard	Known as a sardine when young and a pilchard when mature, these fish can be bought fresh, smoked, and canned in oil, brine or tomato sauce.

Sea bass/striped bass Caught in the North Atlantic and Mediterranean, this white-fleshed fish may be grilled, baked, steamed or stuffed.

Sea bream The pink or white flesh of this medium-oily fish may be steamed, baked, fried or grilled.

Shad A larger plumper type of herring, mostly caught in rivers when they come from the sea to spawn. Shad may be treated like herring.

Skate Caught in the North Atlantic and Arctic, only the wings of this fish are sold. The meaty white flesh is medium-oily and is suitable for poaching, steaming, baking or frying.

Smelt This herring-like fish can be found on both sides of the Atlantic and on the North American Pacific coast. The flesh is firm and ranges from lean to oily and is usually fried.

Sole Dover sole is the finest of the flatfish caught all year round off the coast of Europe, particularly in the North Sea. The white flesh is lean and fine and the fish may be cooked whole or in fillets. Lemon sole can be distinguished from Dover sole by the flesh, which is not as fine, and by the slight lemony smell when it is caught. Both fish may be fried, poached, steamed, baked or grilled.

Sprat/brisling A member of the herring family, it is caught along the coasts of Europe from September to March. The flesh is oily and may be baked, fried or grilled.

Sturgeon This fish is famous for its roe, made into caviar, although its flesh is also of good quality and is best baked, fried, grilled or smoked. It can be found in the Caspian and Black Seas, and in the Western Atlantic from New England to North Carolina.

Swordfish Found all around the world, this fish has a white firm flesh which is medium-oily to oily. It is mainly sold in steaks which may be baked, barbecued or grilled. In Japan the meat is used raw in sushi.

Tilefish A large deep-water fish that can be cooked like cod.

Tuna/tunny/bluefin tuna/albacore/longfin Found in warm waters all around the world, the fish is best eaten in late autumn.

The flesh ranges from light and lean to dark and oily. It can be bought in steaks or, more commonly, tinned and is suitable for grilling or baking. In Japan it is often eaten raw in sushi and sashimi.

Turbot A flatfish found in the Atlantic off the coast of Europe, the Mediterranean and the Black Sea, it is at its best in the summer. The firm flesh is white and medium-oily and may be poached, steamed, baked, fried or grilled.

Whitebait These fish are young (fry) of sprat and herring which are usually eaten whole and deep-fried.

Whiting/silver hake A round-bodied fish of the cod family, caught all year round in the North Atlantic and North Sea and at its best from December to February. The white flesh is lean and bony, and it is best poached, steamed, baked, fried or grilled.

SHELLFISH

Abalone The edible part of this single-shelled mollusc is very firm and needs softening before eating. It is either eaten raw or fried.

Awabi Japanese name for abalone.

Beard The fibrous threads found on mussels which allow them to attach themselves to rocks.

Blue crab Found off the East Coast of the USA, this crab is named after the blue colour of the claws. The meat may be steamed or fried.

Butter clam A large, delicately-flavoured clam found off the Pacific coast of North America.

Clam The flesh of this shellfish, of which there are many varieties found throughout the world, is lean and may be eaten raw, poached, grilled, steamed or baked.

Cockle There are many different varieties to be found around the globe. They are harvested all year round but are best in the summer months. They may be eaten raw, or cooked in their shells.

Coconut crab A large burrowing land crab found throughout the islands of the Pacific and Indian Oceans.

Common crab Found around British coastal waters and from Spain up to Norway, though not in the Mediterranean. Best eaten in the summer, although they may be eaten all year round. The meat can be compared to lobster, but is a lot less expensive, and is removed from the shell after the crab has been boiled whole.

Conch This large sea snail lives in a spirally coiled shell and is found off the coast of Florida and in the Gulf of Mexico. The flesh is tough and therefore needs tenderising by marinating or pounding.

Crawfish Also known as spiny lobster or crayfish, although it should not be confused with the freshwater crayfish. The lean flesh may be baked, fried or grilled. The crawfish may be distinguished from the lobster by the absence of claws.

Crayfish This freshwater crustacean is similar in appearance to a lobster but smaller in size. The flesh may be baked, fried, poached or steamed.

Cuttlefish This cephalopod has an oval body with an internal shell and eight legs sprouting from the head. Normally up to twenty-five centimetres or ten inches long and varying in colour, the cuttlefish has lean flesh which may be poached, steamed, baked or fried.

Dublin Bay prawn Related to the lobster, this shellfish may be found from Iceland to as far down as Italy. The shelled tail meat may be poached, baked, fried or grilled.

King crab Weighing up to eight pounds or three and a half kilogrammes, this large long-legged crab is caught off the coast of Alaska.

King prawn The name given to several species of large prawns found in Australian waters.

Lobster The largest of the crustaceans caught off the coasts of both sides of the Atlantic, it is at its best when weighing between one and two pounds. The lean rich flesh is finer-textured than the crawfish and may be boiled, steamed, baked, fried or grilled.

Mussels Related to the clam and found all over the world in estuaries and on sea shores. They are generally sold fresh in their shells and eaten either raw or steamed in such popular dishes as moules marinière.

Octopus   A seawater cephalopod mollusc with eight tentacles growing out of the head. There are many varieties found around the world in tropical and sub-tropical waters. The edible tentacles may be poached, steamed, baked or fried.

Oyster   Native to the coasts of Europe and America, the many species found vary in size, texture and flavour. Three of the main species are the Pacific, the European flat and the Portuguese. The meat is lean and rich and is traditionally eaten raw with a splash of lemon juice, but may also be poached, baked or fried.

Prawn/shrimp These small, clawless saltwater crustaceans vary considerably in size and have a delicate flavour. Generally in Europe the term prawn is used for those crustaceans over three inches or seven and a half centimetres long, and the term shrimp is used for anything smaller. In the United States shrimp is used for all sizes. When boiled, steamed, fried or grilled the greyish flesh turns a pretty pink.

Quahog   Also known as hard clam or hardshell clam in the United States, it is caught in the Atlantic.

Queen scallop This shellfish is related to the scallop family and is no longer than ten centimetres or four inches. It has rich lean flesh which may be poached, baked, pan-fried or grilled.

Scallop   There are many species found along the European and American coasts but only two basic types, the larger deep-sea scallop and the delicately-flavoured bay scallop. The muscle controlling the shell is the edible part and is lean and rich. It may be pan-fried, poached, baked or grilled.

Shrimp   See *prawn*.

Squid   This seawater cephalopod mollusc can measure up to sixty centimetres or two feet in length and is semi-transparent with eight legs sprouting from the head. The lean flesh may be poached, steamed, baked or fried.

Whelk   Found along the marine coasts of America and Europe, whelks have a spiral shell up to three inches or seven and a half centimetres in length and are best eaten from February to August. The muscular foot is the best part of the flesh which is normally boiled at the place of landing and sold shelled ready to eat with lemon juice and bread.

Winkle   Edible sea snail found off coasts around the world with a shell about one inch or two and a half centimetres in length. The flesh is removed from the shells after boiling and eaten suitably seasoned.

Dairy products

BUTTER

Churned pasteurised cream is used to make butter. Salt may be added to enhance the flavour and this also acts as a preservative. The colour and flavour of butter is determined by the breed of cows from which the milk is taken, their diet, the time of year, the salt content and the way in which it is made. Salted butter has a longer shelf life, although unsalted butter is preferred in baking. Most butter contains approximately 81% fat.

Dairy spread A blend of milk fat from butter or cream and vegetable oils.

Half fat butter With half the fat content, this butter has a higher percentage of water.

Ghee The product of heating butter to rid it of its impurities. Ghee is the yellow liquid left after the sediment has been removed, and traditionally was made from the butter from goat or water buffalo milk. Now ghee is often made from butter from cows. It has a higher burning point than most other oils, which makes it ideal for frying and sautéeing. It is much used in Indian cooking.

CHEESE

Cheese is made from the curds of soured milk from cows, sheep, goats or buffalo, or from milk that has been coagulated with the help of rennet, a curdling substance obtained from the stomach of unweaned calves, or, if vegetarian cheese, from artichokes. Cheese can also be made from whey, the thin liquid left over from cheese-making. Hard cheeses can be kept in the freezer for four months.

Cottage cheese Loose-textured, mild, low-fat soft cheese made up of small white curds.

Curd The thick part of soured or cultured milk when it separates into curds and whey. It is rich in protein.

Fromage blanc This creamy-textured French cheese is made from skimmed milk soured with a culture.

Fromage frais French, bland-tasting, white curd cheese which varies in consistency according to the fat content. It freezes for up to one month.

Quark A German, low-fat, soft cow's milk cheese, similar to a smooth cottage cheese which has a mild flavour.

Ricotta A mild, Italian soft cheese, made from a by-product of the manufacture of cheeses such as Provolone, Mozzarella and Pecorino.

Whey The thin watery part of soured or cultured milk when it separates into curds and whey.

CREAM

Cream is the larger, lighter fat particles that rise to the surface of whole cow's milk, and has a much higher butterfat content than milk.

Clotted cream A speciality of the West Country where large pans of milk are heated, cooled then skimmed of their thick, creamy crust.

Crème fraiche This French cultured cream is similar to soured cream and is used when French recipes specify cream.

Double cream Double cream gives a firmer result when whipped than whipping cream and is easier to use. This cream will not curdle when boiled. It has a 48% butterfat content.

Extra thick double cream This is fresh homogenised double cream, however this cream will not whip successfully.

Extended life double cream This cream is heat-treated, homogenised and vacuum-

HANDY HINT

Home-made soured cream
Stir 5ml (1tsp) lemon juice into 150ml (1/4pt) fresh single cream and leave for 10-15 mins.

sealed in a glass bottle or jar. It will keep successfully for up to three weeks in the fridge.

HANDY HINT

Whipping cream
When whipping cream chill the bowl and utensils for 30 mins before starting to whip.

Half cream Thin pouring cream, usually homogenised and sometimes heat-treated. It contains 12% butterfat and hence cannot be whipped.

Single cream This is pasteurised, fresh pouring cream, which does not contain enough fat for whipping. If adding to hot sauces do not allow to boil as it will curdle. Contains 18% butterfat.

Soured cream/sour cream This is homogenised single cream which is cultured to give a slightly acidic flavour.

UHT cream Available in half, single, double and whipping cream. It has been ultra heat-treated and so has a shelf life of up to three months. When opened it should be treated as pasteurised cream.

Whipping cream This cream doubles in quantity on whipping and has a content of 35-40% butterfat.

MILK

Liquid product from lactating cows, sheep and goats that is used for human consumption. Cow's milk is the most common and is a good source of calcium. Milk is almost always pasteurised  to kill off any potentially dangerous micro-organisms without impairing the flavour, and is available in the following forms.

Buttermilk Originally the sour milk left over from butter making, today buttermilk is usually pasteurised skimmed milk with a culture added to give a thicker consistency.

Condensed milk A thick rich product where water is removed and up to forty per cent extra sugar is added to sweeten and preserve.

Evaporated milk Milk where sixty per cent of the water has been removed.

41

Full-fat milk   Also known as whole milk, it is milk containing all the natural cream which rises to the top of the container.

Homogenised milk Milk treated to evenly distribute the natural cream throughout the liquid.

Long-life milk Milk that has been pasteurised, homogenised and heated to a higher temperature to destroy all bacteria. It tastes sweeter than ordinary milk because the lactose, the natural sugar present in milk, caramelises.

Pasteurisation Heat treatment of milk to kill off any potentially dangerous micro-organisms, without impairing the flavour.

Semi-skimmed milk Milk with approximately fifty per cent of the cream removed.

Skimmed milk Milk with all the cream removed.

UHT milk   After pasteurisation the milk is heated to 132°C or 270°F for one second only, which avoids the caramelisation of the lactose.

YOGHURT

Natural yoghurt is a cultured product made from whole or skimmed milk, containing live bacteria unless it has been pasteurised after manufacture. Yoghurt is available with varying amounts of fat content which give the yoghurt its character, eg. set, creamy, low-fat, very low-fat. Fruit yoghurt has added fruit and will freeze for up to three months. Natural yoghurt will freeze for two months, and both need to be thawed slowly in the fridge.

Greek-style yoghurt Made from either ewe's or cow's milk, and is thick and creamy in texture. Greek-style yoghurt should not be frozen as it separates on thawing.

Bio yoghurt   Made with additional cultures which aid digestion.

Grains and cereals

Grains make up the staple diet of many countries. A grain is an edible seed or fruit from a grass, for example, wheat, rice, maize.

A cereal can refer to the grain itself, and also to any product made from the grain, for example, couscous, oatmeal, flour. The word originates from the Latin *cerealis* from Ceres, the goddess of agriculture in Roman mythology.

BARLEY

Native to the East, barley is the oldest cultivated cereal. It is used as a side dish similar to rice. Barley-flakes are one of the constituents of muesli, and can be made into a nourishing breakfast dish closely resembling porridge. Malt, made from barley, is used for the brewing of beer and the distillation of whisky, and as a nourishing addition to beverages such as Horlicks and Ovaltine.

Barley flour   The flour contains less gluten than wheat, so is usually combined with wheat flour to make bread. It can be used to thicken soups, stews, casseroles and hot pots.

Pearl barley   Dehulled and polished barley grains which may be added to stews and soups or served as a pilaf. Pearl barley is also used to make barley water, which is said to be of benefit to kidneys and bladder.

Bran   The brown outer layer or husk of a cereal, such as wheat and maize, usually separated from the grain during the process of making flour. It is a valuable source of fibre in the diet, and is a main ingredient in breakfast cereals.

BUCKWHEAT

The fruit of a plant native to Russia, where it is known as kasha. The seeds can be boiled in water to produce a side dish similar to rice. The seeds are roasted before making flour.

Buckwheat flour A brownish flour used in Russian blinis and other pancake mixtures such as the Breton crêpes or galettes. It is also used to make noodles, called soba, in the Far East

Corn   See *maize*.

Flour   A meal or powder made from grinding cereal grains or other food, which is used to make bread, biscuits, cakes, pastry, pasta and other products. There are many types of flour, and the type selected will depend on the food being made.

Lotus root flour Milled from dried and powdered lotus root, this gluten-free flour is used in Chinese and Japanese cooking as a thickener for sauces.

MAIZE

A cereal where the grains are large and set on rows on the cob. Also known as corn. It is indigenous to Mexico and is an important source of cooking oil and starch in the form of grain, meal and flour. Cornflakes, cornflour and cornstarch are produced from yellow or white corn.

Cornflour   Flour from the white heart of the maize kernel ground to a very fine powder.

Maize flour/corn meal/cornmeal A gluten-free flour made from North American yellow or white maize. It can be bought as fine, medium or coarse meal which varies in colour according to the colour of the maize. It is widely used to make assorted breads and cakes.

Polenta   Made from yellow or white cornmeal, which is ground coarse or medium and boiled with liquid until it reaches a porridge-like consistency. It can be eaten on its own or used as an accompaniment to meat, fish or vegetarian dishes.

Millet   The small, yellow seed of an annual, gluten-free grass
                 which is widely eaten as a cereal in Africa and Asia, and
                 also used as a source of starch in Russia. It happily
                 grows in both hot and cold climates in the West. It
                 tastes like a cross between semolina and cornmeal
                 when cooked, and makes a nutritious breakfast cereal,
                 which can be cooked like porridge. It is rich in fat and
                 absorbs a vast amount of water as it cooks, but has a
                 short shelf life.

OATS

Native to Central Europe, this annual cereal grass is one
of the richest sources of soluble fibre, which is said to
break down excess cholesterol in the bloodstream. Oats
are a protein and energy food available in several forms.

Whole grain oats Used mainly for processing into other forms,
                 although it is an important energy food for horses.

Jumbo oats   Very large rolled oats.

Rolled oats Oat grains steamed and flattened between rollers. They
                 are used to make porridge and are often called porridge
                 oats, They are also used uncooked in muesli, and
                 cooked in biscuits and cakes, especially delicious
                 flapjacks.

Crushed oats Oat grains that have been put through an oat crusher.

Oatmeal   This comes in three grades, pinhead or coarse, medium
                 and fine. It is made by grinding the grains after the
                 hull or husk has been removed. The cooking time
                 reflects the fineness of the meal.

Oat flour   Flour made by very finely grinding dehulled oats. It is
                 used mainly for oatcakes, scones, bread and biscuits,
                 sometimes in combination with other flours.

Potato flour Made from cooked potatoes that have been ground. It is
                 often used as a thickening agent.

Quinoa   A tiny South American grain, rich in nutrients, high in
                 unsaturated fats but lower in cholesterol than other
                 grains. It is cooked like rice and used in dishes where
                 its subtle flavour provides a good background for
                 stronger flavours.

RICE

The most important of the cereals, it is the grain of a swamp grass grown in paddy fields in hot moist climates.

Basmati rice 'The one of perfume', grown in the foothills of the Himalayas, this fragrant narrow long-grain rice is the longest of them all and hailed as the finest. For rice, which is boiled in water, a narrow thin grain is desirable because it absorbs less liquid than a broader thicker grain. It should be soaked before cooking to remove loose surface starch, which would make the cooked rice sticky.

Brown rice Brown rice has been hulled but the bran layer of the grain remains, providing more fibre and nutrients than white rice, with a fuller flavour and texture. It requires more water and a longer cooking time than white rice.

Converted rice This rice has been par-boiled to remove the surface starch. This process leaves most of the nutrients and vitamins in the grain, unlike other treated white rice varieties.

Glutinous rice There are two varieties, black and white, and the white variety is dehulled in processing. When boiled it becomes sweet and sticky and is therefore used mainly in baking, confectionery and for making beer. Despite its name, this rice is completely gluten-free.

Italian rice A large, round-grained type of rice. The texture of this absorbent rice makes it ideal for the classic Italian risotto. Well-known varieties include Aborio, Carnaroli and Vialone Nano.

Patna rice This is the most versatile and popular of all long-grain rice, and is grown all over the world. The grains are hulled and polished allowing the rice to remain firm and unsplit during cooking.

Pudding rice This short-grained polished rice becomes soft and mushy when cooked, making it ideal for cream puddings.

Rice flour A gluten-free flour ground from both ordinary polished white and brown rice grains, used as a thickening agent and for making noodles. It is a useful thickener for dishes that are to be frozen, as sauces thickened with wheat flour are prone to separating out when reheated after freezing.

Wild rice   Strictly not a true rice, but the seed of a wild grass that is not aquatic. It has a nutty flavour and is usually served mixed with long-grain rice.

RYE

A grain which grows on relatively poor soil in cool temperate conditions.

Rye flour   Commonly used for bread making in Eastern Europe, rye flour is used to make the characteristic pumpernickel and Russian black breads. It is also used in making crispbreads, as well as some Jewish breads, often with caraway seeds.

Sago   The starch obtained from the stem of the South East Asian sago palm. It is most commonly used in sweet milk puddings.

Soy flour   A highly nutritious food supplement which can be added to soups and cakes. It is made from the soya bean, which is not a grain but a pulse.

Tapioca   The starch extracted from the root of the cassava plant and made into pellets. It is most commonly used in sweet milk puddings.

WHEAT

This grain is the main source of the highest quality bread and baking flours and has been grown since pre-historic times. There are many different varieties that fall into two categories, hard wheat, which is rich in gluten, and soft wheat, which is rich in starch. Durum wheat is best known for making pasta.

Bulgar wheat/bulgur wheat/bulghur wheat This is wheat grain that has been par-boiled, then dried with some of the bran removed before being cracked or coarsely crushed. This gives it a lighter, milder flavour when cooked, and it can be baked, cooked as a pilaf or even cooked like porridge as a breakfast cereal. It is also used to make the Lebanese dish tabouleh where the cooked cereal is combined with chopped onion, tomatoes, mint, parsley, olive oil and lemon.

Couscous   A cereal processed from semolina into tiny pellets coated with fine wheat flour. Couscous is cooked by steaming but can also be purchased pre-cooked. It is best known for its use in North African cooking.

Cracked wheat See *bulgar wheat*.

Graham flour Flour milled from the whole grain of the wheat. It differs from ordinary wheat flour because it still contains the bran and wheatgerm.

Kibbled wheat See b*ulgar wheat*.

Semolina   A cereal produced from a milled hard wheat such as durum. The circular granules vary in size and range from cream to pale yellow. It is used to make couscous, pasta, gnocchi and sweet milk puddings.

Wheat flour   There are many varieties, ranging from the all-purpose or plain flour to cake flour or self-raising flour. Plain flour is the refined and bleached product of soft wheat, giving a light short texture in baking. Self-raising flour is plain flour mixed with baking powder, which contains bicarbonate of soda and cream of tartar, and salt. It is used in cake making and is best used up within two to three months as the chemicals in baking powder gradually lose their raising properties.

Wheatgerm   The germ of the wheat grain that is used to grow new wheat plants. It is usually extracted from the grain during flour making. It is very high in nutritional value, and can be bought toasted or raw. The raw variety should be kept in the refrigerator since the oil in the germ quickly goes rancid. It can be eaten on its own or sprinkled on other foods.

HANDY HINT

Make you own SR flour
Add 2$\frac{1}{4}$ level teaspoons of baking powder to every 8oz plain flour and sift mixture twice.

Vegetables

ROOT VEGETABLES

Beetroot
Available all year round. It can be boiled or baked and served hot, cold or pickled. Usually used in soups or salads, the deep pink colour is spectacular.

Black salsify/scorzonera A root vegetable related to the lettuce, native to central and southern Europe. It grows as a tapering root, similar to a parsnip, and its young leaves may be used in salads. It has black skin and a white tender flesh, and it may be boiled on its own or used in savoury dishes.

Carrot
An orange tapering root best in early spring, but available all year round. Can be eaten raw or cooked.

Cassava
It grows as a cylindrical tapering root, native to South America with two main types, sweet or bitter. Cassava is extremely poisonous if eaten raw, and its best known use is in the form of tapioca.

Celeriac
A winter vegetable and a member of the celery family. This special variety is cultivated for its thick tuberous root, and it should be firm and must be peeled before eating. It can be eaten cooked or raw, grated and dressed in a salad.

Chinese artichoke A root vegetable native to the Far East, a pale short and tapering tuber looking like a fat caterpillar. The flavour is delicate and the root may be boiled or fried.

Daikon/mooli A variety of radish with a tapering tuber of up to twelve inches or thirty centimetres in length, widely used in Oriental cooking and is now available in the West. The thin skin and flesh are white, and it can be eaten raw as well as in many cooked dishes.

Dasheen
A vegetable tuber native to Africa, it grows as a cluster of swollen roots with light brown skin and white flesh. It may be cooked on its own or used in savoury dishes and is bland in flavour.

Hamburg parsley This plant is grown for its root, which is white, slender and carrot-like in appearance. Used in soups and stews.

Horseradish A member of the cabbage family, this brown, cylindrical root resembles a thin parsnip. Its flesh is very hard and creamy white and is usually grated before use, traditionally as a basis for the rather hot to the taste sauce to accompany roast beef.

Jerusalem artichoke This tuber ranges from reddish-brown to beige, native to North America but grown in Europe between autumn and spring. It has a nutty taste and is cooked in the same way as potatoes.

Kumara The name given to the sweet potato grown in New Zealand.

Mooli See *daikon*.

Neep Scottish dialect for turnip.

Parsnip A root vegetable native to Europe, it grows as a tapering conical root with green foliage above the ground. The more mature the sweeter the taste, but it is best eaten before the core becomes hard and woody with age. The white flesh may be boiled, roasted, baked or fried on its own or in savoury dishes.

Potato There are many varieties of potato, around eighty in Britain alone, and the skin varies from beige to red. The texture ranges from floury, ideal for mashing, to waxy, which make excellent potato salads, boiled potatoes and gratins. Popular varieties change rapidly as growers develop new disease-resistant types. New potatoes are not a specific type but any potato lifted when small and young, usually between June and August, while maincrop old potatoes are dug up from late summer onwards and can be stored through the winter.

Radish A root vegetable of the mustard family, it has a crisp texture and a peppery taste which ranges from strong to mild depending on size and type.

Salsify Related to the lettuce, this slender, tapering root has tender flesh and creamy coloured flesh. It may be

HANDY HINT

Cooking baked potatoes quicker
Insert a skewer to conduct the heat to the centre.

eaten raw, cooked in savoury dishes or on its own as a vegetable.

Swede   Native to Europe, it has a swollen root in the shape of a ball. The skin is purple in most cases, with the dense flesh being yellow and slightly sweet to the taste. It may be grated and eaten raw in salads but is more often cooked as a vegetable or used in savoury dishes. In North America and parts of the north of Britain it is known as a turnip.

Sweet potato   There are many varieties of this vegetable tuber that is part of the morning glory family native to South America. The most common varieties available in this country have an elongated potato shape tapering at one end with the flesh either yellow or white. It is either cooked as a vegetable or used in savoury or dessert dishes.

Taro/coco   This brown-skinned white-fleshed cluster of swollen stems is bland in flavour and cooked as a vegetable or in savoury dishes.

Turnip   The turnip grows as a swollen, cylindrical root topped with green leaves. The smooth skin ranges in colour from green to purple to white and the root is at its best when eaten young. It may be grated and eaten raw or cooked as a vegetable.

Yam   Mostly native to Africa, the yam has an elongated potato shape with slightly reddish-brown or brownish-pink skin, and white, pink or yellow flesh and is either soft or firm. Yam should never be eaten raw, but cooked as a vegetable or in a savoury dish. A few varieties of the yam resemble the sweet potato and are sold as such, but the two vegetables are not of the same botanical genus.

SHOOT VEGETABLES

Asparagus   There are about twenty varieties, green being the most common, followed by the white variety preferred by the French and Italians. The asparagus spear should be

picked when very young as the stalk can become woody and the buds can open out.

Bamboo The conical shoots of the bamboo are sold fresh in the Far Eastern markets but can be bought here in tins. The shoots are cut when they reach six inches long, and are used raw or lightly cooked.

Cardoon Native to the Mediterranean, the roots and stalks are similar to celery and eaten raw or cooked as a vegetable.

Celery There are two types of celery, Pascal, which has green leaves and stem and the golden which has yellow leaves and white stem. Celery is used raw in salads, cooked in savoury dishes or as a vegetable. The distinctive flavour of celery is used in celery salt, delicious with boiled quail's eggs.

Fennel A celery-like shoot which has an aniseed flavour. The leaves are used as a herb traditionally with fish and the bulbous leaf stalk is used either raw in salads or cooked as a vegetable. It is in season from autumn to early summer.

Globe artichoke An edible thistle which belongs to the daisy family. The edible parts are contained in the green, cone-shaped head. The artichoke head consists of three different parts: the outer petals, which have a partly edible fleshy base; the inedible central choke which is a mass of fine bristles; and the tender base which is the main edible portion, located under the choke. Young artichokes may be eaten raw, the older ones are boiled and served hot or cold with a dressing. Artichoke bottoms may be bought tinned.

Samphire A member of the carrot family, it grows in rocky coastal areas and has strongly flavoured, fleshy green leaves with yellow flowers.

Seakale The wild seashore plant is gathered for its white stems and eaten like asparagus.

Aubergine/eggplant From the same family as the tomato, it is available all year round. The tender, glossy skin is usually purple in colour, but is also found in white or green. The flesh is creamy and peppered with tiny seeds, and it can be either baked, grilled or fried as a vegetable or used as part of a savoury dish.

Avocado This buttery, creamy-fleshed green or purple-skinned fruit has a large central stone and a mild distinctive flavour. All avocados are pear-shaped. The flesh is eaten raw with a dressing or used in savoury dishes.

Breadfruit This large round green-skinned fruit contains a pulp which is eaten as a vegetable, traditionally roasted. It can also be used in sweet dishes and when baked has the smell of freshly baked bread.

Capsicum/pepper/pimento The shape may be squat like a tomato, elongated or tapered to resemble a chilli. The most familiar are the sweet green varieties which ripen to being red or yellow in colour. There are also black, orange or variegated varieties.

Chilli pepper The small green or red conical peppers are the fiery chillies. Bird, cayenne or Thai chillies are very thin varieties with a fiery taste. The small green jalapeno varies from hot to very hot. Green anaheim chillies are a larger variety and have a mild taste.

Jackfruit The skin of this large, oval fruit is yellowish-brown, rough and prickly and the fruit can take up to six months to ripen after being picked. The sweet, juicy flesh is divided into pockets and can be eaten raw or cooked as a vegetable.

Plantain The plantain has a green skin and is generally larger than its relative, the banana. The skin is difficult to remove, its flesh is firm and starchy and it is mainly eaten boiled, baked or fried as a vegetable.

> HANDY HINT
>
> **Avocado**
> Place the stone on or near the cut avocado or avocado mixture to prevent it turning brown.

Tomatillo   Belonging to the tomato family and related to the cape gooseberry, this fruit vegetable resembles a walnut-sized green tomato enclosed in a thin papery wrapper. It has a firm texture with the flavour of a tart apple, and is used in Mexican cuisine in salsas or savoury dishes.

Tomato   There are many varieties of this fruit including beefsteak, cherry, green and plum. Initially green in colour this fruit turns red when ripe with many different shapes and sizes according to variety. The tomato may be eaten raw in salads or used in many cooked dishes.

SQUASHES

Butternut   One of the winter squash group usually eaten in winter, this yellow thick-skinned vegetable is similar in shape to a marrow with a bulbous end. The orange flesh, which contains a central core of flat seeds, is smooth and has a slightly nutty taste. Eaten as a vegetable on its own or in savoury dishes.

Courgette   A small variety of the marrow family with either dark green or yellow skin. The flesh is watery and crisp and may be eaten raw or cooked as a vegetable.

Cucumber   Varieties range from the small, ridged cucumber to the smooth-skinned cucumbers known as hothouse. They can be pickled, salted, used in savoury dishes, salads or cooked as a vegetable.

Custard squash   A summer squash with a floury taste which is best eaten very ripe. It can be steamed, boiled, baked or stuffed, and the skin, seeds and flesh may all be eaten.

Golden nugget squash   Orange with greenish flesh, this summer squash is normally eaten when young as a vegetable or in a savoury dish. When mature, it can be peeled, boiled and mashed with butter and seasoning.

Marrow   An edible summer squash, firm and heavy, and up to about twelve inches or thirty centimetres in length. Used as a vegetable or stuffed with a savoury mixture and baked in the oven.

Pumpkin The shape of this winter squash is usually round and the flesh orange. The flesh contains edible seeds and is used in either sweet or savoury dishes.

Spaghetti It is shaped rather like an American football, oval with flattish panels. The yellow skin is smooth and thick, and the flesh is pale yellow and stringy, like spaghetti, when cooked.

BULBS

Garlic Available all year round, it grows in bulbs each containing individually wrapped cloves. The flavour is strong and pungent.

Leek A winter plant native to Europe and a member of the onion family. Tall and cylindrical in shape, the colour varies from very pale green at the root to dark green where the leaves end.

Onion Most types of onion begin as tender green shoots and develop into bulbous swellings wrapped in a golden papery skin.

Pickling onion Picked when the bulb is first formed and is usually used for pickling.

Red onion Red-skinned onion which has a mild and sometimes sweet taste. The red-tinged flesh is attractive in salads.

Shallot Less pungent than the onion, it is mainly used in sauces. The elongated variety has a stronger flavour.

Spanish onion Mild and sweet tasting, this onion is available all year round.

Spring/salad onion/scallion A member of the onion family picked when young before the bulb matures. The onions are sold as spring onions or salad onions from midwinter to midsummer. The ripe onion may be used raw or boiled, fried, steamed or braised.

HANDY HINT

Onions
When slicing or chopping, leave the root on to prevent the layers slipping.

Bean sprouts A sprouted mung bean, mainly used in Oriental cooking.

Broad /fava bean May be eaten fresh or dried, although fava beans are usually shelled. Very young pods may be cooked whole and eaten.

Corn/sweetcorn/maize Eaten as a vegetable in its immature state, and used fresh, dried, frozen or canned.

Dwarf beans A hybrid French bean which has little or no side strings.

French beans Immature, long thin pods which only need to be topped and tailed before cooking.

Green beans A general term for beans grown with edible pods.

Mange-tout/snow pea The large flat mange-tout pods are peas in the pod picked before maturity which can be eaten raw or cooked with only the tops removed.

Monguete A Spanish variety of French bean.

Okra/ladies' fingers The pod is the fruit of an annual plant native to Africa. They are eaten fresh, cooked, canned or dried as a vegetable or in a savoury dish.

Pea Edible round seeds contained in the green pod of a climbing plant. The peas are removed from the pod by shelling and, depending on age, may be eaten raw or cooked.

Runner beans This long, thin green pod containing pink beans is best picked when young and tender, cooked whole or sliced, and eaten as a vegetable or cold in salads.

Sugar snaps Similar to the mange-tout, the sugar snap has an edible pod but is picked when the peas have matured and swollen slightly.

Yard beans A green vegetable which is grown long and thin and mainly used in Far Eastern cuisine.

HANDY HINT

Sweetcorn
Cook in unsalted water as salt toughens the kernels.

Broccoli There are two types, the green broccoli and the purple, both are a variety of cauliflower and members of the cabbage family. Broccoli consists of long green stalks with branching shoots ending with clusters of immature flowers.

Brussels sprouts They grow as a number of small, individual clusters of green leaves resembling cabbages along a stalk. The smaller and tighter the sprout the better it tastes.

Cabbage The vegetable consists of a short thick stalk and a large, multi-layered leafy head in green, white or red. White cabbage is suitable for eating raw, while the green and red cabbages are more often cooked.

Cauliflower Cauliflower consists of a sturdy stalk topped by a tightly packed, fleshy white head of immature flowers surrounded by green leaves. It may be eaten raw, boiled, steamed or roasted, in salads or in savoury dishes.

Kale/collard There are many varieties of crinkly and smooth-leaved kales. This winter vegetable is rather coarse in texture therefore best simmered and served with butter.

Kohlrabi Either purple or green, the thickened stem is edible and has a turnip taste. It grows as a swollen, round bulbous stem from which sprout thin stems topped with leaves. It may be eaten raw, grated in a salad or cooked as a vegetable.

Pak choi This plant does not form a heart and is similar to a spinach leaf. It can be eaten raw in salads but is best known for its use in stir-fried Far Eastern dishes.

Romanesco This decorative vegetable is a pale green variety of cauliflower and reminiscent of a domed cluster of mosques, each with its own peak.

Savoy cabbage A dark green cabbage with heavily veined leaves.

Spring greens A young cabbage harvested in the spring when immature and before it has grown a heart!

Swiss chard/sea kale beet It grows as a cluster of stalks topped with crinkly oval leaves and is harvested before maturity when the leaves are more tender. Both the leaves and the shoots are used. It is available from spring to winter, and is best steamed and eaten as a vegetable.

Bamboo leaf Used in Oriental cooking to wrap food in prior to cooking.

Batavia endive/escarole Variety of endive that has much broader leaves than the curly endive.

Beet greens A mild, earthy leaf which adds colour to salads. These leaves can also be cooked like spinach and eaten as a vegetable.

Belgian endive This small, elongated tightly-packed vegetable is harvested when still at the shoot stage and about ten centimetres or four inches long. The colour of the leaves is creamy-white with pale greenish-yellow tips, and it can be eaten raw in a salad or braised as a vegetable.

Boston A good example of a butterhead lettuce with light, loosely-packed delicate leaves. This lettuce is popular in the States.

Callaloo/Chinese spinach A spinach-like vegetable.

Chicory Available all year round, this curly leaf has a bitter, slightly sharp taste. The outer leaves are dark green and a pale greenish-yellow at the heart. Used mainly as a salad leaf, but can also be braised and used as a vegetable. Also known as curly endive.

Ciccorio See *radiccio.*

Corn salad/lamb's lettuce/mâche Grown mainly in France and Italy, it grows as a cluster of dark green leaves which are picked when young. This winter vegetable has a slightly bitter taste and is used either as a garnish or a salad leaf.

Cos This lettuce has elongated leaves, which are a deep green on the outside and lighter in colour at the centre, where the leaves are sweeter and more tender. Mainly used in salads but can be braised as in petit pois à la française.

Cress Eaten at the seedling stage, this European plant is usually found in combination with mustard, which has a warm, sharp flavour, and is used in salads and as a garnish.

Curly endive Available all year round, this curly leaf has a bitter, slightly sharp taste. The outer leaves are dark green and a pale greenish-yellow at the heart. Used mainly as a salad leaf, but can also be braised and used as a vegetable. Also known as chicory.

Dandelion   A wild plant with a bright yellow flower. The leaves are used in salads or as a vegetable, and should be eaten before the plant flowers, as they become bitter. The roots make a coffee substitute.

Endive/escarole See *curly endive* and *Batavia endive*.

Frissee   See *curly endive*.

Good King Henry A perennial herb which is sometimes used as a substitute for spinach.

Heart of palm/palm hearts The buds of the palm tree which resemble the heads of cabbage and are eaten as a vegetable. Available tinned in the UK.

Iceberg   A ball-shaped lettuce, pale green in colour with crisp, closely packed leaves, with little taste.

Lamb's lettuce See *corn salad*.

Land cress/American cress/winter cress This winter leaf cultivated for its slightly peppery taste and mainly used in salads.

Lettuce   There are three main types of lettuce: cos, known also as romaine; crisphead, which has a tight solid heart; and butterhead or cabbage which has loose coarse leaves. They are available all year round now and are mainly eaten in salads but can also be braised and eaten as a vegetable.

Lollo biando A loosehead lettuce with light-green curly leaves and a mild taste.

Lollo rosso Another loosehead lettuce with red-bronzed curly leaves.

Mâche   See *corn salad*.

Mizuna   This feathery, delicate salad leaf is native to Japan. Picked when young, it has a mild peppery taste.

Mustard & cress Mixture of mustard and cress leaves, grown from seed and used in salads.

Nasturtium The leaves of this annual

HANDY HINT

Salad leaves
Don't cut with a knife as this will turn the ends brown. Tear the leaves.

plant, which taste similar to watercress, can be shredded and added to salads. The brightly coloured flowers are also edible and can be added to salads.

Nettle A perennial plant, which can be cooked as a purée, used in soups or brewed to make tea and beer.

Oak leaf lettuce This lettuce has bronze-green oak-shaped leaves and has a slightly more bitter taste than cos.

Purslane These green fleshy leaves, which when young are suitable for use in salads, have a mild but sharply distinctive flavour.

Radicchio/ciccorio These miniature reddish-pink lettuces have a slightly bitter taste and add a splash of colour to any salad.

Rocket Also called roquette, rucola or arugula, this young dark green leaf has a pungent peppery taste that gives a lift to any plain green salad.

Romaine American name for cos.

Seaweed Any vegetation that grows in seawater. Some varieties are edible, and may be eaten fresh from the sea or, more commonly, dried.

Sorrel It has large, green, fleshy leaves, which have a slightly bitter taste. It can be used as a substitute for spinach in soups or sauces.

Spinach The younger dark green leaves are best used in salads where their tender sweet leaves are delicious. The older, larger and more pointed leaves are best washed thoroughly to remove any grit and gently steamed or cooked with butter and black pepper and served as a vegetable.

Vine leaf This leaf of the vine is best known in Near Eastern cooking where it is stuffed with rice and minced meat and called dolmades.

Watercress A member of the nasturtium family, dark green bunched sprigs of watercress make a wonderful garnish. It has a distinctive peppery taste and is used in sauces and soups as well as in salads.

Webb's Wonderful One of the most successful commercially-grown lettuces, it is ball-shaped with dark green, firm and slightly crinkled leaves.

Bay bolete An edible mushroom with a smooth bun-shaped brown cap. It is slightly sticky when young and has a short slender stem.

Blewitt It has a pale brown cap with a short stem which has a blueish appearance. It should be thoroughly cooked to eliminate any possible harmful substances.

Boletus See *cep*.

Button This cultivated common mushroom has a white cap, is brown underneath, and is picked before the head has opened.

Cep/boletus This mushroom has a smooth brown cap with a white to greenish-yellow underside. It has a thick short stem which is white when young, turning brown as it ages. It can be bought dried as well as fresh.

Chanterelle With a distinctive yellow colour, this mushroom has the odour similar to an apricot. When young it has a small round flat cap which develops an upturned wavy edge and a deep hollow in the middle. It is available dried, fresh or canned.

Chestnut These are strong-flavoured mushrooms which are brown in colour with a firm texture. They are known as cremini in the United States.

Chinese Available dried from Chinese food shops. These mushrooms have a very strong and distinctive flavour.

Cup A common mushroom where the cup has partially opened.

Enoki A Japanese mushroom that grows in clumps of long thin needle-like miniature mushrooms, used in Oriental cooking.

Field mushroom Found in meadows from late summer to autumn, they have a white cap.

Flat A mature common mushroom where the cup has fully opened to reveal dark brown gills.

HANDY HINT

Mushrooms
Wipe rather than peel cultivated mushrooms as the best flavour is just under the skin.

61

Giant puffball Found in woods and fields from August to October and only edible when young, firm and white.

Girolle A small chanterelle mushroom found in France.

Horn of plenty/trompette des morts Trumpet-shaped mushrooms that look dirty, and have a strong and earthy taste.

Horse mushroom Known in France as boule de neige, the horse mushroom is similar to the puffball when young, but when it has matured the creamy white cap opens up to reveal chocolate-coloured gills.

Morel This is not a true mushroom, and is easy to recognise by its brown sponge-like cap, pitted with hollows in which the spores are produced. Available in spring through to early summer, but also can be purchased dried or canned.

Oyster Mainly cultivated now, the colour varies from oyster grey to white, to yellowish-brown, to almost black. The stalks are short and tough, the gills are white and the flesh is thick and fleshy, best eaten when young.

Parasol Available from July to November in sandy meadows, it resembles a parasol with tiny scales on its cap. It has a strong meaty smell and should be picked young, but avoid eating the stalk as it is tough and fibrous.

Porcini Dried cep.

Potabella A mature chestnut mushroom, ranging from three to eight inches, or seven and a half to twenty centimetres in diameter, brown in colour with a stronger taste than the common mushroom.

Shiitake Found cultivated and wild in Japan and China, this edible mushroom is widely used in Oriental cuisine. Grown on logs, they are dried in the sun and should be soaked in warm water for twenty minutes before use.

Straw These small conical mushrooms are grown in China on wet rice straw beds and are sold fresh or dried.

Truffle An edible fungus which grows just below the surface of the earth on oak tree roots. Truffles are the rarest of fungi. They have a rich, woody mould-like flavour and a little goes a long way. The Italian white truffle is small in comparison and has a more pronounced flavour than the French black Perigord truffle.

Pulses

Pulse is the generic name for all dried peas, beans and lentils. Drying preserves them, allowing long storage. Generally they need to be soaked before cooking, preferably overnight. They are a valuable source of protein.

Aduki bean   A native of Japan, it is small and red with a white striped ridge. It is cooked in the same way as all dried beans but is much sweeter, and its flour is used for making cakes and pastries in Japan and China.

Black bean   A shiny, black bean with creamy flesh that is tender and sweet tasting. It is the staple of soups and stews in South and Central America, often baked with ham or other cured pork, and flavoured with garlic, cumin and chilli in Brazil.

Black fermented Chinese bean Soybeans or other beans preserved in salt and used in meat and vegetable dishes.

Black-eyed bean This white bean with its characteristic black spot, although native to China, has become popular in the American South, where it is traditionally served with pork.

Blue pea   Probably the most tasty of the several varieties of dried peas, the pea retains its shape after cooking and has a floury texture.

Borlotto bean This Italian pink mottled bean is used in casseroles, cold in salads and puréed into dips which have a beautiful creamy consistency.

Boston bean   North American name for haricot bean.

Broad bean   Broad beans become brown when dried and are also known as fava beans. They are strongly flavoured and are commonly used in Egyptian falafel. These are deep-fried patties made with soaked and pounded dried beans, flavoured with garlic, onions, cumin, fresh coriander and parsley.

Butter bean   Also known as lima beans, these come in small and large sizes and are usually a pale buttery colour, although sometimes they are a very pale shade of green. In Central and Southern America, where the bean is grown, it is eaten fresh as a vegetable, although for export purposes the bean is dried and used as a pulse. All varieties of this bean must be boiled vigorously for the first fifteen minutes to destroy toxins found in the outer skin, which if eaten can prove harmful to the human body.

Cannellini bean   An oval or kidney-shaped white bean, with a firm texture, first grown in South America but now grown in Italy.

Chick-pea   There are several sizes of this dried pea, native to Western Asia. The larger peas are a better buy as they do not need such long soaking. They can be served in casseroles, soups and stews and are the main ingredient of Arabian houmous, which also contains olive oil, tahina, garlic and lemon juice.

Fava bean   See *broad bean*.

Flageolet   A small, green variety of haricot bean, native to America. They can be used fresh or dried and are also available pre-cooked and canned. Traditionally flageolet beans are eaten with lamb in France.

Ful medames   Native to the Middle East and golden yellow in colour, the white variety is called ful nabed. Ful medames have given their name to the national dish of Egypt in which they are baked with eggs, cumin and garlic.

Haricot bean   A small, greyish-white oval bean used in casseroles and soups. It is the bean used in canned baked beans.

Lablab   These hard-skinned beans, commonly eaten throughout Asia and the Middle East, must be shelled before cooking.

Large white bean   A large flat variety of the haricot bean, these beans are used in stews and casseroles.

Lentil   Lentils can be yellow, green, orange, red or brown. The dark green French lentils, also known as puy, vary in size and are considered to be the best of their type. Yellow, brown, red and orange lentils, native to Asia, are more commonly known by their Indian name as various types of dhal. Indian brown lentils are red lentils from which the seedcoat has not been removed and they become a purée when cooked. The orange lentil is the only pulse that does not need to be soaked before cooking. It may be sold whole or split, and it also becomes a purée when cooked.

Mung bean They are now chiefly used in the West for sprouting purposes, ground into flour in India, and used as the basis of some Chinese and Japanese noodles.

Pigeon pea bean Native to Africa, also eaten in India and the Caribbean, they take their name 'pea' from their shape and size.

Red kidney bean Varying in colour from dark pink to burgundy, this sweet tasting bean is most commonly identified with the Mexican dish, chilli con carne.

Rice bean Named after their rice-like taste, these beans are grown in China, India and the Phillipines.

Soybean This bean, native to China, has many uses. It can be cooked fresh or dried in stews, sprouted, turned into soy paste, bean milk, bean curd or tofu and textured meat substitute.

Split yellow/green pea The green variety is sweeter than the blue pea and is commonly used in the traditional English pease pudding. Like the split green pea, the yellow variety makes excellent soup, and is very good served as a vegetable dish with ham.

Urd bean A black-skinned bean which is widely grown in India and the Far East. It may be used whole, skinned or split.

Fruits

BERRY FRUITS

Barberry A small elongated red berry containing a few small seeds. It is best made into preserves as it is too sour to eat raw.

Bilberry See *blueberry*.

Blackberry This berry is available in late summer to early autumn and is eaten fresh or in pies or made into preserves.

Blackcurrant A small, almost black, round and juicy berry. Best known for its use in cassis, but is also delicious in pies, puddings and preserves.

Blueberry In season in mid-summer, this small, round blue berry may be eaten fresh, in pies or in desserts.

Bounceberry See *cranberry*.

Boysenberry A hybrid of a blackberry, raspberry and a loganberry, this red berry may be eaten fresh or in preserves.

Bramble See *blackberry*.

Cape gooseberry This berry is wrapped in a papery skin which when pulled open reveals a golden cherry-like fruit. May be eaten raw or made into a preserve.

Cloudberry Similar to a round golden-coloured blackberry with a sweet honey and baked apple taste. This berry is native to North America.

Cowberry A member of the cranberry family which grows wild throughout Northern Europe, North West America and parts of Asia.

Cranberry This winter berry is red in colour and too sharp to eat raw but is used in numerous sweet and savoury dishes, and as a juice.

Crowberry This black fruit is similar to the cranberry and may be used as a substitute.

Dewberry	A close relative of the blackberry only the fruit is larger and juicier.
Elderberry	The fruit of a tree or shrub, this small, round, seeded fruit turns black when ripe. This berry makes an excellent wine or cordial and is also used in pies with other fruit or in preserves.
Gooseberry	This oval, green, hairy fruit is best used in cooked dishes because it has a very sharp taste. The larger and more colourful types are softer and sweeter to taste and may be eaten raw.
Hawthorn	The berries of this plant are used to make jams and jellies.
Huckleberry	This berry is related to the blueberry and is similar in appearance.
Juneberry	Similar to a blackcurrant and used in the same way.
Ligonberry	Also known as the lingonberry, this arctic cranberry is found in parts of Scandinavia and is used in desserts and sauces.
Loganberry	A cross between a blackberry and a raspberry and a dull red colour. Slightly larger than a blackberry, with a slightly sweet-sour taste, this berry is used fresh, in pies and in preserves.
Mulberry	Similar in appearance to an elongated blackberry but paler, this very fragile fruit is best eaten on its own or in fruit salads. The white berry is not as good as the red.
Naseberry	This brown-coloured fruit is only edible when ripe and has a delicious taste of brown sugar.
Physalis	See *cape gooseberry*.
Raspberry	Related to the rose family, this deep red fruit is delicious and best eaten fresh in the height of summer. It is also available in white and black cultivated varieties.
Redcurrant	A red translucent berry with a sour taste, best eaten in sweet or savoury dishes as it is a little too tart to eat fresh.
Rose hip	A member of the rose family, the hip can be orange-red to dark red and is best used in syrups and preserves, but combines well with other fruit in desserts.

Rowanberry This pectin-rich orange berry is too bitter to be eaten raw, but is excellent in preserves.

Strawberry A native of America, this bright red berry is delicious eaten fresh especially with cream, and is available all year round but is best from late spring to early summer.

Tayberry Similar in appearance and use to the loganberry, it is larger and tastes less sour.

Veitchberry Similar to the loganberry and is used in the same way.

Whitecurrant This berry is less acid-tasting than the redcurrant and may be eaten on its own or used in preserves.

Whortleberry See *blueberry*.

Wineberry A relative of the blackberry which grows in China and Japan, the wineberry is sweet and juicy and may be eaten on its own.

Worcesterberry An American gooseberry, the black fruit may be used in a similar way.

Youngberry A hybrid of the loganberry and the dewberry, it resembles a dark red loganberry and may be eaten raw or used as a substitute for the blackberry or raspberry.

CITRUS FRUITS

Bitter orange See *Seville orange*.

Blood orange Sharper-tasting than an ordinary orange with a reddish skin and orange and red flesh.

Calamondin/China orange A cross between a lime and a kumquat, this fruit is no larger than four centimetres or one and a half inches in diameter and has a golden-red skin. Often grown as a houseplant, it is suitable for use in preserves and pickles.

Clementine A cultivated version of the tangerine. It is slightly larger with a smoother skin than the mandarin and is often seedless.

Grapefruit One of the larger members of the citrus family, there are two main varieties; those with yellow flesh and those with pink flesh. The pink grapefruit is sweet enough to eat without sugar.

Kumquat/cumquat A small orange-like fruit with sweet skin and slightly bitter flesh. It may be eaten fresh or made into preserves.

Lemon The fruit is too acidic for most people's taste to eat fresh, but it has numerous culinary uses in both sweet and savoury dishes.

Lime Native to South East Asia, the skin is thin, there is little pith and the fruit is more aromatic than the lemon. Used in sweet and savoury dishes and also used in making pickles and preserves.

Mandarin Smaller than the orange with a very loose skin which is easy to peel.

Mineola A cross between a grapefruit and a tangerine, with bright orange skin and a protrusion that gives it a bell-like shape. It has a slightly spicy taste.

Navel This sweet orange is distinguished by the 'navel' on its underside which contains a small secondary fruit.

Orange There are two main types of oranges, sweet and bitter. Sweet are suitable for eating fresh, and bitter are better suited to making marmalades.

Pomelo/shaddock Similar to the grapefruit but larger with a dimpled skin. The sweet flesh can be eaten on its own or used in sweet or savoury dishes.

Satsuma This cultivated fruit is one of the smallest of the citrus fruits and has no pips.

Seville orange Due to its bitter taste, this orange is best used in marmalades and savoury dishes.

Tangelo A hybrid of the grapefruit and tangerine.

Tangerine Native to China, this fruit has a skin which is very easy to peel and contains many pips.

Topaz A hybrid of an orange and a tangerine, with a skin which is easy to peel.

HANDY HINT

Oranges and lemons
A juicy medium-sized orange will give approximately 60mls or 4 tablespoons of juice and a lemon 45mls or 3 tablespoons of juice. Warm slightly before juicing and this will get more juice out.

HANDY HINT

Lemon
Lemon juice can be used in recipes instead of vinegar, except when pickling.

Ugli	This fruit is another hybrid of the grapefruit and tangerine, and is the size of a large grapefruit.
Valencia	A spherical-shaped, thin-skinned sweet orange with juicy flesh.

EXOTIC FRUITS

Akee	The fruit is the same size as a peach, eaten when it reaches maturity and has a red skin. When fully ripe the skin splits to reveal three poisonous black seeds surrounded by white flesh. Only the flesh is edible and it has a delicate flavour similar to an avocado.
Alligator pear	See *avocado pear.*
Apple banana	It is a very small banana and has a flavour reminiscent of pineapples and apples.
Asian pear	The fruit resembles an apple, with golden coloured skin and white, crisp juicy flesh which tastes like a pear. It is native to Japan.
Banana	The fruit of a plant native to the Far East and available throughout the year. Usually eaten raw, bananas are also delicious baked or flambéed. The inedible skin turns from green when unripe to yellow when the flesh is ready to eat.
Barbados cherry	The bright red skin darkens to almost black when the fruit is ripe. It has a single seed surrounded by juicy and sweet flesh. It can be eaten raw or used in preserves.
Carambola	See *starfruit.*
Chinese cherry	See *lychee.*
Chinese gooseberry	See *kiwi fruit.*
Custard apple	Native to Central America, the size and colour of the fruit varies. It has a skin patterned like a fir-cone which sometimes turns black when ripe. The sweet flesh is milky-white, has a custard-like texture and is studded with black seeds.
Durian	Native to Malaysia, it has an oval shape and can weigh up to four and a half kilograms or ten pounds in weight. The skin is thick and sticky, and dark yellow

when ripe. The yellowy flesh is divided into four sections and contains up to six seeds. The Malaysians rate the durian as the king of fruits.

Golden passion fruit It is slightly larger and has a more pulpy flesh than the closely-related purple passion fruit.

Granadilla Related to the passionfruit.

Guava It varies in size from a walnut to an apple, when ripe the skin is light yellow and the flesh, varying from white, to yellow, to pale pink is juicy and contains small seeds. It may be eaten as a fruit or used in pies and preserves.

Hairy lychee See *rambutan*.

Hog plum From the same family as the mango, it is plum-shaped with a yellow skin and has delicious yellow or red flesh surrounding a large stone.

Kiwi fruit This fruit is oval in shape with brown hairy skin and green soft flesh speckled with tiny black edible seeds. It tastes similar to a melon or a strawberry.

Longan Native to India, this fruit is related to the lychee and rambutan, hence its similar appearance and taste to the lychee.

Loquat This fruit is plum-shaped with a yellowy-orange, slightly downy skin similar to an apricot. The fragrant flesh can be anything from white to orange, has up to four brown seeds and may be eaten raw.

Lychee Native to Southern China, this round fruit with its rough, brownish-red skin can be easily peeled to reveal translucent and firm white flesh enclosing a small, brown kernel. It has the delicate flavour of a sweet muscat grape and may be eaten on its own or purchased canned in syrup.

Mango The smooth skin of this fruit turns from green to yellow-red as it ripens. The flesh is pale orange in colour and has the most delicious slightly perfumed taste.

Mangosteen The same size as a small orange the fruit has a deep purple shell with juicy creamy-white flesh arranged in segments.

Nashi See *Asian pear*.

Papaya   See *pawpaw*.

Passion fruit   The fruit of the passion flower, purple in colour, is about the size of an egg. When ripe the skin is slightly wrinkled, inside the pulp is sweet and juicy and is eaten raw.

Pawpaw   This large pear-shaped fruit has a yellow rind with yellow to slightly pink flesh with a large central cavity containing many small black seeds. Unripe fruit may be used in a similar way to squash, and when eaten raw the ripe flesh is best when splashed with lemon or lime juice.

Persimmon   Native to Asia and North America, it is shaped like a large tomato with yellow-orange flesh when mature. This 'apple of the Orient' is only eaten when very ripe and has deep-orange soft flesh.

Pineapple   The skin of this tropical fruit, which changes in colour from green to yellow as it ripens, is rough and resembles a honeycomb. The fruit is topped with a crown of green leaves. The firm, fibrous juicy flesh varies from a pale to golden-yellow according to the variety, the latter being the sweetest.

Pomegranate   The size of a large orange, the fruit has a hard yellow skin tinged with red-brown and the white seeds are found in juicy pink flesh. This fruit is eaten by cutting it in half and easing out the pink flesh and removing the seeds which are quite bitter.

Prickly pear   This pear-shaped fruit has a tough thin skin covered in barbed prickles. As the fruit ripens the skin changes from green to greenish-orange. The fruit has a seed-filled white, yellow or orange flesh which is sweet and juicy when ripe, and the seeds are edible if soft.

Rambutan   The size of a Victoria plum, this fruit is covered in soft spines and, when ripe, is red in colour. The creamy-white flesh is slightly perfumed, with a central brown seed which is inedible.

Rose apple   Native to the Far East, this small, pink and white pear-shaped fruit grows in clusters, tastes similar to the English apple, and is full of seeds.

Sharon fruit   A recent relative of the persimmon fruit, developed in Israel in the Sharon Valley. The skin is orange in colour as is the flesh, both of which are edible, and it is the size of a large apple. It may be eaten in a similar way to an apple but should be eaten while still feeling hard as the fruit deteriorates once over-ripe.

Sour sop   A member of the custard apple family and native to tropical America, it is heart-shaped and has a green spiny skin. It is not as tasty as the other members of this family, but it is very juicy and makes a good basis for desserts and drinks.

Star fruit   Shaped rather like a banana with five deep grooves running lengthways so that when it is cut across the fruit resembles a star. It is a translucent yellow with a thin edible skin and a sweet acidic taste when fully ripe.

Sweet sop/sugar apple See *custard apple*.

Tamarillo   A relative of the tomato family, native to South America, it is egg-shaped, about two inches or five centimetres long and has a glossy tough red or yellow skin. The flesh is slightly lighter in colour and is divided like a tomato containing dark, edible seeds, and tastes similar to a cross between a tomato and a cape gooseberry. The fruit, when blanched and skinned, may be eaten raw or used as part of a dish or in preserves.

FIRM FRUITS

Apple   There are many varieties of
apple, broken down into three groups, the wild crab apple, the cooking apple and the cultivated dessert apple.

Crab apple
These small, sour apples grow wild or in gardens and are ancestors of all modern varieties of apple. They are rarely eaten raw due to their size but make a wonderful pink clear jelly, delicious on crumpets!

Cooking apple
The foremost British cooking apple is the Bramley, not usually eaten raw due to its acidity but used for making chutney, in desserts or savoury dishes. When selecting cooking apples always choose a hard crisp-textured apple.

Dessert apple

There are many dessert apples on the market including Cox's Orange Pippin, Worcester Pearmain, Golden and Red Delicious and Granny Smith.

Medlar   From the same family as the apple and pear, the fruit is about the size of a small apple with a very prominent calyx which gives it the appearance of a rosehip. This fruit is only edible when over-ripe and the flesh is brown. When ready to eat the flesh can be scooped out of the brown skin with a spoon and the seeds discarded, but the medlar is more commonly used in preserves.

Pear   There are nearly as many varieties of this fruit as the apple, varying in colour, shape and size. The best known English eating variety is the William's pear, in season in late summer, with Comice and Conference being available later in the year. Cooking pears are harder and less perfumed.

Quince   These golden-yellow, small pear-shaped fruits originate from central Asia. They are usually used to make aromatic jam or jellies, and traditionally in England are made into a cheese, which is then dried and eaten as a pudding.

Rhubarb   Technically a vegetable, the edible stem is a bright pink when young, ripening to a deep red or greenish-red when mature. It may be eaten raw when young, but is best cooked on its own with a sweetener or with other fruits. The leaves should not be eaten as they are poisonous.

SEEDED FRUITS

Cantaloup melon This melon, a member of the musk melon family, has a warty ribbed skin with a sweet fragrant pale orange flesh, and is in season during the summer months.

Charentais melon The French version of the Cantaloupe melon with a deep orange flesh.

Fig   A relative of the mulberry, the shape of the fruit depends on the variety and can vary from spherical to an elongated pear shape. The skin may sometimes appear ribbed and once ripe may be eaten as well as the flesh. The colour of the skin varies from pale green to a deep purple, and the sweet, soft seeded flesh varies similarly.

Galia melon   A small round melon developed in Israel with a yellow bark-like skin and sweet green flesh when ripe.

Grape   The fruit is round or oval with a thin skin and pulpy sweet flesh, with or without seeds, and it grows in elongated bunches on the vine.

Honeydew melon This winter melon has a yellow skin with a pale green flesh and a delicate taste that contrasts well with port or muscatel.

Muscat grape Available all year round, the fruit may be translucent green, scarlet to purple or a deep blue. They all have seeds and a distinctive perfumed flesh.

Musk melon   A group of melons distinguished by the network pattern on the skin which is either green or yellowy-orange with green to salmon-pink heavily perfumed flesh. More commonly known in the United States as a cantaloup melon.

Ogen melon   A yellow smooth-skinned cantaloup hybrid with delicate pale yellow flesh.

Pineapple melon Originally from Japan, this new variety of Israeli melon has a hard rind striped in light and dark green with golden flesh interspersed with brown seeds. It is deliciously crisp, quite sweet and tastes faintly of pineapple.

Seedless grape They have much less tannin than other varieties, with sweet juicy flesh and no seeds.

Watermelon   They are much larger than the other varieties of melons and have sweet red flesh and black seeds. The skin can have deep green rinds or may be striped on a light green background, such as on the Tiger watermelon.

Apricot
Native to China, the tender skin of the apricot varies from a pale to a very rich orange according to the variety. The sweet flesh surrounds a single stone and is much firmer and drier than that of the peach, making apricots ideal for cooking as well as eating fresh. They are in season through late spring and summer.

Cherry
The cherry, a relative of the plum, comes in hundreds of varieties from black to red to a pale cream with a rosy tinge, and is generally classified as either sweet or sour. The thin shiny skin surrounds juicy flesh with a central stone. The Morello cherry is best known for its use in cooking while the Napoleon, Bigarreau and Frogmore Early are delicious eaten fresh.

Damson
A type of plum, oval in shape with a tough blue-black skin and yellowish-green flesh surrounding a central oval stone. The damson is too sour to eat raw but makes wonderful gin and jam.

Date
Known as 'bread of the desert' in the Middle East, this elongated fruit has a brown skin with a paler brown sweet flesh surrounding a single slender stone. The best dates are plump with wrinkly non-sticky skin and a fudge-like texture. Exported dates are sometimes dried or semi-dried, but the fresh varieties are more readily available in the shops now and well worth trying.

Gage
Related to the plum family, these fruits are relatively small in size, with a sweet flesh and delicate perfume. Two of the most common varieties are the greengage and the golden mirabelle.

Nectarine
This fruit has a smooth shiny orangy-red coloured skin with anything from white to red flesh, surrounding a central stone. It tastes somewhere between a plum and a peach, having a similar texture to the plum. It is firm, sweet and more juicy than the peach.

Peach
The soft downy skin varies in colour from white to orange flushed with red, with flesh that is tender and

juicy. Peaches are normally classified as being either freestone, where the flesh does not cling to the stone, or clingstone where it does.

Plum
Related to the rose family, the fruit may be oval or spherical depending on the variety. The skin may be any colour from yellow to black with flesh that reflects the colour of the skin. The sweeter varieties are eaten raw while the more sour varieties are used in cooking, especially for making preserves.

Sloe
A member of the plum family, it is round in shape and about one centimetre or a little under half an inch in diameter. The black skin covers a sour tasting yellowish-green flesh surrounding a central stone. It is not eaten raw, but is used in flavouring gin and in preserves.

Dried fruits

Drying fruit not only preserves summer fruit for winter months but also concentrates the sugar content of the fresh fruit giving it a sweeter richer taste which lends itself very well to baking and desserts. It can be eaten on its own, used in fruit cakes, in stuffings, on cereals or topped with custard, yoghurt or cream.

Apples An old-fashioned way of preserving this fruit from when cold storage and modern techniques of preservation were unknown.

Apricots These dried fruits are often more flavoursome than the fresh fruit.

Bananas The fruit is split lengthways and the process of drying in the sun intensifies the delicious taste of the banana. Dried banana is also sold in chips, often mixed with other dried fruit and nuts and eaten as a snack.

Candied peel This consists of candied, or cooked in sugar syrup, pieces of citron, lemon and orange peel. It is used in cakes and teabreads.

Crystallised fruit This is candied fruit that has a coating of granulated sugar.

Currants Sun-dried seedless grapes which get their name from Corinth in Greece. They are mainly used in baking.

Dates There are three types of dates, dry, semi-dry and the more popular soft. The Middle Eastern Deglet Noor, Hallawi and the Khadrawi are the main varieties and may be eaten raw or used in baking.

Figs The yellow Smyrna fig from Turkey and the juicy Mission fig from the USA are the most famous varieties. They may be eaten on their own, served with Parma ham or used in puddings and for baking.

Glacé The term glacé on fruit refers to the coating of syrup put onto the fruit, for example, glacé cherries.

Pears   The popular Bartlett pear is halved, sulphured and sun-dried. They are used in baking or on their own.

Prunes   These are whole dried plums, the finest being from Agen and Tours in France. They are traditionally eaten with game, goose and pork and are used in puddings and ice creams. Soaking in water overnight causes them to become plump again.

Raisins   Sun-dried fruit made from the sweet Spanish muscat grape. Now raisins are grown in other regions, predominantly California. They are eaten as a dessert fruit and used in various sweet and savoury dishes.

Sultanas   Sun-dried seedless grapes originally from Smyrna in Turkey, which gave the fruit its name. They are now grown in other parts of the world and used in many sweet and savoury dishes.

Nuts

Acajou   See *cashew*.

Almond/sweet almond Can be eaten fresh from the shell or roasted and salted. Almonds are used whole, flaked, chopped or ground in a variety of dishes, and they are the main ingredient in marzipan.

Babassu   Hard-shelled nut from a tall palm, native to north-east Brazil, which yields a valuable oil.

Beech   Only edible when roasted, and tastes like a combination of a hazelnut and a chestnut. They also yield a fine oil.

Betel   The bitter-tasting nuts and leaves of the plant, together with lime, are chewed to stimulate the saliva glands and aid digestion in south-east Asia.

Bitter almond Similar to the sweet almond in shape, but the presence of benzaldehyde makes this nut poisonous if eaten in quantity.

Brazil   These nuts are clustered inside a large coconut-shaped shell grown on a tall tree in Brazil, surprisingly enough! The shell of each individual nut is shaped like an orange segment and is dark brown in colour, and the white kernel is rich in oil.

Butternut   Related to the walnut family, this edible oily nut is native to North America.

Candlenut   Native to the Orient, this nut is shaped like the hazelnut, grows on the candleberry tree, and is used in Malay cooking as a thickening agent.

Cashew   This crescent-shaped nut, grown in abundance in India, has a mild sweet taste. Often cashews are roasted and salted.

Chestnut   The fruit of a tree native to southern Europe, the chestnut may be eaten on its own shelled and skinned, boiled, dried, roasted, or preserved in syrup.

Cobnut	See *hazelnut*.
Coconut	The fruit of the coconut palm. The husk of the mature coconut is covered in a brown fibrous covering, the white flesh is eaten fresh or dried, and the milk can be drunk on its own or used in cooking.
Filbert	See *hazelnut*.
Ginkgo	This creamy-fleshed small nut is used in Oriental cookery.
Green walnut	Young walnut which is picked and pickled before the shell has had time to mature. Pickled walnuts are delicious with cheese.
Groundnut	See *peanut*.
Hazelnut	This thick-shelled nut, native to Europe and North America, is most commonly used in deserts or confectionery but can be eaten on its own.
Indian	See *pine nut*.
Kemiri	See *candlenut*.
Kernel	The edible part of the nut.
Macadamia	This round, skinless, creamy-coloured nut is native to Australia, and is also cultivated now in Hawaii.
Monkeynut	See *peanut*.
Paradise	A more delicately-flavoured nut similar to the Brazil nut with a thinner shell.
Peanut	This small bean-like nut grows in pairs in brittle shells beneath the ground on thin twigs. They may be eaten raw, or roasted and salted. They are also made into peanut butter.
Pecan	Similar in shape to the walnut but slightly more elongated and milder in flavour. These nuts may be eaten raw or used in cooking.
Pignoli/pinoli	See *pine nut*.
Pine nut/pine kernel	Cream-coloured seeds of the Mediterranean stone pine tree. Delicious in salads and used in sauces for pasta and as an ingredient in pesto.

HANDY HINT

Skinning hazelnuts
Grill until the skin splits, place in a bag and rub until the skins have come away.

Pistachio Pale green in colour with a subtle flavour, this nut grows inside a small hard shell which splits naturally at one end when ripe. Best eaten raw and also used as a flavouring for ice cream.

Sapucaya See *paradise nut*.

Shanghai Roasted peanuts covered in a crisp savoury coating and served as a snack.

Shea The nuts of this tropical African tree are used to make shea butter.

Shell The hard outer part of the nut, usually inedible.

Spanish chestnut/sweet chestnut Widely-cultivated chestnut tree that produces edible sweet nuts.

Walnut The wrinkled brown edible kernel of this nut grows in two halves and is enclosed in a hard brown shell. Young walnuts are green in colour and may be pickled or made into ketchup.

Herbs

Angelica   The leaves and stem of the plant are used. It is commonly candied and used as cake decoration.

Basil   The leaves are best used fresh when they have a flavour similar to cloves, when dried they have a curry taste. Use with oily fish, roast lamb, chicken, duck and tomatoes.

Bay   These leaves are used in stocks and form one of the ingredients for bouquet garni. They are an important flavouring in béchamel sauce and are used to garnish patés.

Bergamot   Both the flowers and the leaves are used, fresh or dried in teas and tisanes.

Borage   The leaves have a mild cucumber flavour, and they are traditionally used in Pimm's and fruit cups.

Burnet   The fresh or dried leaves of this herb are used in soups, salads, cordials or casseroles. It has a slight nutty flavour with a hint of cucumber.

Camomile   There are many different varieties of this herb. The dried flower heads are dried and used to make a relaxing tea drink.

Caraway   More commonly known for the use of its seeds in baking and cheese, the leaves are also delicious in salads.

Chervil   The leaves and fine stems of this herb with a delicate flavour are used mainly with fish and shellfish.

Chive   This herb belongs to the onion family, hence the oniony taste. The leaves are used primarily for garnishing soups and salads.

Comfrey
The leaves can either be used fresh in salads or dried in teas. The dried root is used as flavouring for country wines.

Coriander
Also known as Chinese parsley or cilantro. The leaves, roots and seeds have a strong flavour and are used primarily in Eastern cuisine.

Curry
These leaves are a basic ingredient for curries and are used either fresh or dried.

Dill
A member of the parsley family, the feathery leaves are used either fresh or dried in salads, sauces or on vegetables, and are especially good accompanying fish, cucumber and lamb. The seeds are also used for flavouring fish dishes.

Fennel
The fresh leaves, seeds and dried root have an aniseed taste and are excellent with fish and with roast lamb.

Fenugreek
The leaves are an important ingredient in Indian cooking, and are used either fresh or dried. The seeds are also used in chutneys and pickles, and ground as an ingredient in curry powder.

Garlic
See under *bulb vegetables*.

Hop
The young shoots of this plant are used like asparagus, and the matured shoots are dried and used for brewing beer.

Hyssop
The oil distilled from the leaves is a main ingredient used in some liqueurs, most famously Chartreuse. The flowers and leaves have a minty taste and can be used either fresh or dried.

Lemon balm
The lemon-scented leaves are used fresh in salads, etc. or dried in tea.

Lemon grass
A thick-stemmed fibrous grass with citric oils which give a lemon flavour. It is used mainly in salads, fish dishes and soups.

Lemon verbena
The leaves are primarily used dried in tea, but they can also be used fresh in cooking.

Lime leaves
The glossy leaves of the evergreen South East Asian makrut tree are used like bay leaves to give Asian dishes a citrus flavour.

HANDY HINT

Making mint sauce
Add sugar to leaves to make it easier to chop.

Lovage	The leaves, root and seeds are all used, most commonly in soups and salads.
Marigold	The flowers are used fresh in salads or dried to give colour in food dye.
Marjoram	The leaves can be used dried or fresh, mainly in meat casseroles and in stuffings. A favourite with tomatoes and can be substituted for oregano.
Mint	The leaves are used fresh or dried. There are many varieties, including spearmint, applemint and peppermint. It is best known for mint sauce which is excellent with lamb, and preferably made with fresh leaves.
Myrtle	The fresh leaves may be used as a substitute for bay leaves, and are especially good in lamb and pork dishes.
Nasturtium	The leaves and petals are used fresh in salads and have a distinct peppery flavour. The seeds are also used in cooking.
Oregano	The leaves can be used either dried or fresh, most notably in Italian savoury dishes.
Parsley	There are many varieties of this herb, most commonly the curly and continental varieties. Parsley is used in many recipes, and is a very popular garnish.
Rosemary	The leaves of this aromatic plant are used either fresh or dried, and are an excellent accompaniment to lamb and oven-roasted potatoes.
Sage	There are many varieties of this pungent herb. The leaves are used either fresh or dried, mainly with pork or in stuffings.
Sorrel	The large, green leaves have a slightly bitter taste. They are mainly used in soups and salads, and can be a substitute for spinach.
Summer savory	Summer savory has a more delicate mint flavour than winter savory, and is used to accompany grilled meat, fish and egg dishes. It is also especially good with runner beans.

> **HANDY HINT**
>
> **Parsley**
> Eat parsley to get rid of the smell of garlic on the breath.

Tarragon   A fragrant aromatic herb which complements meat, fish and poultry. Only the leaves are used.

Thyme   Thyme has a strong taste and is commonly used dried or fresh in bouquet garni, and as an ingredient in stuffings for meat and poultry.

Winter savoury The peppery flavour of the leaves is excellent as a seasoning in cooking, and the herb can be used dried or fresh.

Woodruff   This herb has a distinctive taste and can be used fresh or dried. When dried, the leaves are usually used to flavour champagne, Benedictine and fruit cups.

Spices and seeds

Ajowan   These seeds have a strong taste of thyme and are used widely in Indian cookery.

Allspice   Also known as Jamaica pepper, these dried berries taste and smell like a blend of cinnamon, nutmeg and cloves, hence the name.

Anise pepper   Primarily used in Oriental cookery, the dried red berries are hot and spicy.

Aniseed   Also known as sweet cumin, these seeds can be ground into a powder and are commonly used in Indian cookery or Western baking.

Annato   These hard, red dried seeds are largely used in South American cooking, and the orange outer shell of the seed is also used as a food dye.

Black mustard seed   These hot seeds are used in Indian cookery.

Black peppercorn   See *peppercorn*.

Caraway   These seeds are primarily used in baking and are related to aniseed. They are also used as the basis of kummel liqueur.

Cardamom   These pods are the dried fruit from a plant native to India and part of the ginger family. They can be white, green or black, the white pods having been laid out to dry in the sun. Used in Scandinavian and Asian cookery and also in pickling spice and marinades.

Cassia   Cassia bark is popular in Oriental cookery. This spice is commonly mistaken for cinnamon and can be used whole or ground.

Cayenne pepper   This hot spice is created from the ground pods of dried chilli peppers.

Celery salt   Celery salt is a blend of ground celery seed and flake salt. It is an excellent seasoning for fish, poultry and eggs, and is especially good with quails' eggs.

Chilli powder   This very hot and spicy product from ground chilli peppers is used mainly in sambals, curries and Mexican dishes.

Chinese five spice   Best used to accompany beef or pork dishes, this Chinese spice powder consists of equal parts of ground cinnamon, cloves, fennel seed, anise pepper and ground star anise.

Cinnamon   This dried aromatic spice can be purchased as bark, quills or as ground powder. Native to Sri Lanka, it is generally used to flavour Western sweet dishes and savoury dishes in the East.

Clove   The dried unopened bud of a small bushy tree. The clove is normally used whole, but can be ground into a powder and used in sweet or savoury dishes. It is well known for its flavouring of spiced alcoholic cups.

Coriander seed   Coriander seeds have a mild, sweet, spicy orange flavour and are perfect for Chinese cooking. They can be used ground or whole.

Curry powder   A classic blend of various ground fine spices producing anything from a mild to a very hot curry depending on the ingredients.

Dill seed   The seeds taste like caraway and complement fish dishes well.

Fennel seed   These dried aromatic seeds have a slight aniseed taste and are used in both sweet and savoury dishes.

Fenugreek   These seeds of a plant found in Asia are dried and ground into powder, and commonly used in Indian cookery. The flavour is slightly bitter.

Galangal   Galangal has a ginger flavour and is used mainly in curries. It is the dried root of a Chinese plant.

Ginger   This root stem from South East Asia can be used whole, sliced or ground. It is often used in sweet Western dishes.

Horseradish   The pungent root of the horseradish plant. See *horseradish relish* and *horseradish sauce*.

Juniper	The ripe berries of this evergreen shrub are dried and used primarily in game casseroles. Juniper berries are also a main ingredient in gin.
Liquorice	The dried root of this plant has a sweet, bitter taste, and is used primarily in confectionery and drinks.
Mace	This is the outer net-like covering of nutmeg and is known as the blade. These blades are pressed flat and dried and can also be ground.
Mustard	The ground black and white seeds from either the yellow or the white mustard plant. The black seeds are hotter than the white.
Nigella	Also known as wild onion seed or black cumin, these peppery seeds are often used in baking.
Nutmeg	This spice has a warm, aromatic sweet flavour, and is an important ingredient in milk puddings, sauces and cheese and vegetable dishes. The dried kernel can be freshly grated or used already ground.
Paprika	This dried ground pepper from South America varies in colour from orange to red, and in taste from sweet to mildly hot.
Peppercorn	These are dried berries and are available in the following forms.
	Green Grown on the pepper vine native to Asia, these unripened berries should always be freshly ground.
	Black These are green peppercorns dried in the sun. The best flavour is from freshly ground pepper.
	White These are milder than black peppercorns, and are produced by removing the dried outer layer of the green peppercorn.
Pickling spice	A combination of chillies, black peppercorns, black mustard seeds, allspice, mace, cloves and ginger. It is used in pickles and chutneys.
Poppy seed	There are two types of seed, blue-black and white, and both are used in Jewish and Indian cookery.
Saffron	Saffron is the most expensive spice to buy and is used both as a spice and a food dye. The dried stamens, from a particular species of crocus, are dark orange and have a slightly exotic mild flavour. It is used mainly in Middle Eastern and Mediterranean cookery.

Sesame seed   More commonly known for its oil, the black or white seeds of the sesame plant are ground in the Eastern Mediterranean to produce halva and tahina. The white seeds are also used roasted in salads, and for baking in the West.

Star anise   The dried star-shaped fruit of a Chinese evergreen tree. The seeds are contained in the pod, and both are used in Eastern cookery.

Sunflower seed   These are roasted in their husks and eaten as a snack, rich in protein, or scattered on salads.

Tamarind seed   Though this is referred to as a seed, it is the inside of the fruit, including the pulp, of the tamarind tree that is used, mainly in curries.

Turmeric   The root stems of this plant are dried and then ground to produce a fresh-tasting, mild yellow-orange powder. It is used sometimes as a poor man's substitute for saffron.

Vanilla   The dried pod of a orchid native to Central America, used either whole, as an infusion, or split open with the seeds scraped out and put into the dish. It is used mainly in sweet dishes, and is also available in the form of an essence.

Tools and utensils

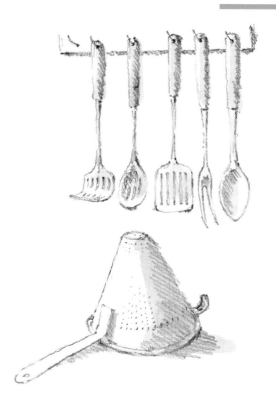

Tools and utensils

Apple corer   A cylindrical hollow piece of stainless steel with a sharp bottom edge, which is placed over the core of the apple and firmly pushed through. When removed the core of the apple is retained within.

Bain-marie   The culinary term for a vessel half filled with hot water, in which saucepans or dishes containing sauces, custards, etc. are placed so that their contents are kept at nearly boiling point without actually boiling, thus preventing curdling or reducing.

Baking sheet   A flat metal sheet for oven use which should be made from heavy-duty steel to prevent warping under intense heat.

Balloon whisk   This wire whisk is mainly used for whisking egg whites, sauces, etc. and is specially designed to ensure a better blend for less effort.

Blender   An electric liquidiser with a goblet. A set of rotary blades, attached to the base of the goblet, quickly reduces most ingredients to a smooth consistency.

Blow torch   This can be used to caramelise the tops of puddings and desserts, such as crème brûlée, allowing greater control of the heat than when put under the grill to brown.

Boat mould   A shaped mould used for pastry cases with sweet or savoury fillings.

Bulb roaster   Pipette with a rubber bulb to draw the fat from roasting into the pipette. This can then be basted onto the meat by squeezing the bulb.

Casserole dish   A reasonably heavy enamel, earthenware or glass dish with a tight-fitting lid used for oven-cooked recipes.

Charlotte mould   A straight-sided round mould used mainly for a Charlotte Russe or Apple Charlotte but also useful for making steamed or baked puddings and for setting sweet and savoury creams.

Chicken brick A porous earthenware dish with a tight-fitting lid designed to cook a whole chicken in its own juices in the oven using no added fat. Before use the brick should be soaked in water for fifteen minutes.

Chinois A cone-shaped sieve made with a fine mesh of stainless steel, ideally made from one piece of metal, and used for the fine puréeing of foods, such as redcurrants to make a coulis.

Chopping board Traditionally made of wood, used for chopping and cutting a variety of foods. When cleaning, the board should not be soaked in water as it will warp. Colour coded PVC boards are now widely used to avoid cross contamination.

Cocotte A small earthenware ovenproof dish of single portion size. It is also called a ramekin.

Colander A metal or plastic perforated basket with a firm standing base and handle. Mainly used for washing or draining vegetables, salads, etc.

Conical strainer A cone-shaped metal sieve used for straining sauces and liquids. It controls the liquid so that it can be directed more easily into another container thereby avoiding spillage. A Tammy strainer is the same shape but made of gauze rather than steel.

Cooling rack A raised stainless steel wire rack used for supporting cooked cakes and pastries when removed from the oven to cool. It allows the steam to escape, thus preventing a soggy finished product.

Couscousière An open steamer used for cooking couscous over a pan of stew.

Dariole mould A mould mainly used for sweet or savoury creams, shaped like a bucket and made in varying sizes.

Daubière An earthenware pot with a lid which is used to cook rich French stews known as daubes.

Digester The original word for pressure cooker.

Dredger See *sifter*.

Egg separator A simple device consisting of a small metal bowl with a slot in the side to allow the egg white to run out while retaining the yolk in the bowl.

Egg slicer The stainless steel wires on these slicers are useful for cutting hard-boiled eggs cleanly without the yolk crumbling.

Fish kettle A large oblong-shaped pan fitted with a strainer, which allows the whole cooked fish to be removed with ease.

Fish slice A flat, rectangular slotted tool with a long handle used for removing or turning food in one piece from the dish or pan. It also drains excess liquid or oil from the food.

Flan ring A round metal ring used for baking flans, where there is either a separate base for easy removal of cooked pastry cases or the baking sheet itself is used as the support for the pastry.

Food mixer/food processor An electrically driven machine that minces, purees, slices, grates, chops and makes bread or pastry by use of a blade or disc fitted onto a central rotating spindle. It is advisable not to fill the bowl more than half full. It does not whip egg whites effectively.

Fruit squeezer See *juice extractor*.

Funnel A cone-shaped tube with an extended base at the narrow end used for decanting liquids into narrow-necked bottles or jars It can be made from plastic, stainless steel or glass.

Garlic press An aluminium or stainless steel press with a coarse mesh used to crush cloves of garlic.

Grater   An implement for breaking solid food into small particles by rubbing it against a perforated serrated edge surface. It is ideally made from stainless steel in a square or cylindrical shape that will stand on a work surface without slipping. Generally the grater should have different grating surfaces suitable for different jobs, although some small graters are made for one specific task, eg. a nutmeg grater.

Gratin dish   Traditionally made from copper in France, but now available in porcelain, enamelled cast-iron and stoneware. Used for any dish that requires browning off at a high temperature, eg. lasagne or a vegetable gratin.

Griddle   A thick iron plate which is heated until very hot and used to cook griddle cakes and scones.

Icing bag   See *piping bag*.

Jelly bag   A cloth bag used to strain the juice of cooked fruit, after which it is boiled with sugar to make a jelly. It is also used to strain clarified stock to make consommé.

Jelly mould   This may be made from metal, plastic, glass, porcelain or earthenware, and is used for setting sweet or savoury dishes. The mould may be plain or ornamental.

Juice extractor Models range from the simple conical-shaped squeezer where the citrus fruit is cut in half and manually pressed and rotated to extract the juice, to the electrically operated juicers which take away all the hard work. The more sophisticated models have filters to separate the juice from the pith and pips.

Kitchen scissors Large general-purpose scissors with modified parts to handle specific tasks, eg. removing metal caps from bottles, levering lids off tins, and gripping screw lids to unscrew them more easily.

Knives   There are many different types of kitchen knives designed for specific tasks. Three types of steel are used. Carbon steel is sharp and can be re-sharpened but it discolours and rusts easily and needs to be thoroughly dried after use. Stainless steel blunts easily and is difficult to re-sharpen but does not easily rust or discolour. High carbon stainless steel has the advantages of both as it can be re-sharpened and does not easily rust or discolour but it is the most expensive.

Boning knife
This should have a rigid blade, and the bigger the joint of meat the larger and more rigid the blade should be.

Bread knife
This should have a long serrated-edge blade, which should not be used for anything other than its proper purpose.

Canelle knife
Has a small V-shaped blade which is used to remove the skin from fruit and vegetables, often to make a decorative pattern.

Cheese knife
This has a curved blade with a double-pointed end which is used to pick up the cut cheese.

Chopping knife or cook's knife
A heavy-bladed knife made in varying sizes. The handle should be almost as heavy as the blade as this gives the knife a good balance and makes it easier to use. Used for chopping and general use.

Carving knife
This has a straight narrow blade with a rounded or pointed end.

Filleting knife
A thin flexible blade used for filleting and boning fish.

Grapefruit knife
A double-edged serrated knife which is curved at the end to loosen the flesh in the grapefruit.

Hachinette/mezza luna
Crescent-shaped double-handled blade used to chop herbs finely.

Palette knife
A blunt round-bladed knife made in varying sizes. Used for turning food while cooking, releasing cakes from their tins, and transferring biscuits, etc. from baking tray to cooling rack.

Vegetable knife
A small knife with a blade of three to five inches long used for chopping vegetables.

Ladle A large long-handled spoon with a cup-shaped bowl. The spherical design of the bowl allows soups and stews to be served without spillage.

Larding needle A long hollow needle with a clasp at the top end to hold bacon fat. The needle inserts the fat into animal flesh in order to keep it moist during cooking.

Loaf tin Rectangular tin with deep sides, available in different sizes, used for baking bread, cakes or terrines.

Madeleine/shell mould A shaped mould used for baking cakes of that name, made in varying sizes.

Mandolin An implement for slicing and paring vegetables, made from stainless steel blades set in slots in an oblong framework. The thickness of the slices is controlled by adjustable blade settings.

Measuring jug A jug with measurements printed on or punched into the surface of the jug. Toughened glass jugs are the best choice as they can withstand boiling liquids, whereas plastic jugs may distort and cause inaccurate readings. Stainless steel and china jugs are opaque and therefore are not as easy to read.

Measuring spoons Sets of calibrated spoons that provide an accurate measure for ingredients. They include the standard teaspoon, dessertspoon and tablespoon and sometimes additional measures such as a half-teaspoon.

Meat tenderiser A wooden mallet with a flat, grid-shaped front used for beating meat to tenderise and/or flatten it before cooking.

Melon baller A small spoon-like instrument for scooping melon flesh into small balls for use in fruit salad.

Moule à manqué This is a deep cake tin with slightly sloping sides and is primarily used for cakes which are to be iced. The sloping sides allow the icing to easily coat the cake. It can also be used for cream sweets that are turned out and masked with cream.

Mouli sieve A stainless steel rotary sieve with a range of discs which can give a coarse, medium or fine finish to sauces, soups or puréed vegetables.

Pastry brush A small round or flat brush used to coat the surface of uncooked pastry with beaten egg for a glaze, or to glaze fruit with warm jam.

Pastry/biscuit cutters These metal cutters are used to cut shapes out of pastry and other dough-like mixtures for baking. Most commonly they are circular with a straight or fluted edge, but they are also made in assorted shapes and sizes, eg. stars, diamonds, hexagons, or gingerbread men.

Pepper mill There are many different styles on the market, but arguably the classic wooden mill with a removable lid for easy filling and a steel grinding mechanism is the best. Pepper should always be freshly ground to ensure its pungency.

Pestle and mortar A short, fat club-shaped instrument, the pestle, and a bowl, the mortar, are used together to crush and grind ingredients to a paste or powder. They are usually made from unglazed porcelain or marble.

Petite marmite A lidded earthenware pot used to serve French soups.

Piping bag A cone-shaped nylon bag into which a nozzle is placed at the narrower end. The contents of the bag are forced through by twisting the top of the bag. There are many types of nozzle available, ranging from small fluted ones used for the intricate icing on cakes to larger round ones used to pipe out éclairs and meringues.

Potato masher A device with a perforated flat metal base which is repeatedly pressed into cooked vegetables to break them up into a smooth homogenous mass. It is traditionally made of stainless steel which will not break under the pressure of mashing potatoes or root vegetables.

Potato peeler A tool with a metal blade for removing the skin from potatoes and other vegetables. The swivel-bladed peeler allows the skin to be speedily removed in either

direction, whereas the fixed blade peeler is used in the same way as a knife. Both versions have a pointed end for digging out the potato eyes.

Potato ricer This consists of a perforated metal container in which potatoes or other cooked vegetables are placed. A flat metal plate is then forced into the container by means of a handle. Makes the best mashed potato!

Pots and pans Are made in a variety of sizes and from a range of materials.

Aluminium pans
These pans conduct heat well and evenly. They are inexpensive and can be used on any type of cooker.

Cast iron pans
These pans are very heavy and are good conductors of heat. They are particularly good for long slow cooking.

Copper pans
The *crème de la crème* of saucepans. They are very popular with professional chefs but are high maintenance. These pans are excellent conductors of heat, and the tin lining prevents the copper from coming into contact with the food which could cause a toxic reaction if the food contains an acid.

Enamel-coated pans
Enamel-coated pans are heavy-based and conduct heat evenly. They are much heavier than aluminium pans, but, as the enamel does not retain the smell of food, much more hygienic. As they chip and scratch easily, metal spoons and metal scourers should never be used and too fierce a heat should be avoided.

Non-stick coated pans
Take care not to overheat these types of pans as the surface will gradually break down. Always clean with care as this surface scratches easily.

Stainless steel pans
Generally the bases of these pans are made from aluminium or copper which conducts the heat evenly. These pans are durable and easy to clean.

There are a number of pans which are designed for particular tasks in the kitchen.

Double saucepan
A two-part saucepan, the lower half being filled with boiling water, and designed to allow the food in the upper half to cook without the application of direct heat or moisture.

Frying pan
Traditionally made from cast-iron with a heavy base which is ideal for retaining heat, but now made from other materials, such as aluminium and stainless steel. The non-stick frying pans are also good but do not last as long.

Milk pan
This has a lip for easy pouring and sometimes a wide rim to prevent liquids from boiling over. They are available in non-stick which is ideal for making scrambled eggs or sauces.

Pasta pan
A stainless steel pan with a perforated inner basket which makes it easier to remove and drain the pasta.

Preserving pan
A large heavy saucepan with sloping sides, traditionally made of tin-lined copper but also now made of stainless steel or lined aluminium, used for making jams and other preserves.

Sauté pan
Rather like a deep frying pan, shallow enough to fry and deep enough to hold liquid for cooking.

Steamer
These are ideally made from stainless steel with one or two compartments with a perforated base which stack on top of each other above a bottom pan which holds the boiling water. Chinese bamboo steamers are very much cheaper but are less durable.

Poultry shears Similar to garden secateurs, the coiled spring gives added strength for cutting through bones. One blade is usually serrated to give a good grip and the pointed end of the blades enables access to awkward places.

Pressure cooker A lidded saucepan made of thick aluminium in which food is cooked under pressure. The lid has a pressure gauge and a safety valve. Food is cooked through raising the pressure of the steam generated inside it from a little boiling water. The increase in pressure and temperature speeds up the cooking process for anything placed within it. Instructions should always be read carefully before using.

Ramekin Small earthenware, ovenproof dish of single portion size. It is also called a cocotte.

Roasting tin A large metal tray with sides for roasting meat, game and poultry. Heavy gauge stainless steel is the best material as it will not warp or rust.

Rolling pin A wooden, porcelain or marble pole available in various sizes, most commonly around five centimetres in diameter and twenty-five to fifty centimetres long. It is used mainly for rolling out pastry, biscuit and scone mixtures.

Rotary whisk A hand-held implement used for beating, whisking and aerating, consisting of metal loops which are rotated by a cog wheel driven by a small handle.

Salad spinner An empty container with a removable basket which is spun around by turning a handle on the lid. The water from the washed salad is removed by centrifugal force without any damage to the leaves.

Salt mill Usually made in the same style as its accompanying pepper mill, it reduces coarse sea salt to a smaller, more palatable, size.

Sauce spoon This resembles a large, flat-bowled teaspoon and is sometimes used as a setting in a restaurant. It is used to eat the sauce accompanying fish, meat or poultry dishes.

Scales The old fashioned balanced scale is a simple mechanism operated on a see-saw principle which is very accurate. The electric battery-operated scales have a digital display but are not very accurate for small amounts weighing under one ounce or thirty grams. The accuracy of the spring balance scale may be put out after use, so it is important to purchase one where the scale may be readjusted for accuracy.

Sieve   A fine-meshed tool with a handle used for straining, rinsing, draining, sifting, sieving or puréeing food.

Sifter/dredger A container with a perforated lid used to either dust a work surface with flour or to sprinkle cakes and puddings with sugar or cocoa powder.

Skewer   Long, thin, round or flat-bladed rods of metal onto which chunks of uncooked food are threaded. Wooden skewers are also used but these are not reusable and do not conduct the heat into the centre of the food.

Skillet   North American term for a lidded frying pan.

Skimmer   The spider skimmer is a fine wire mesh basket on the end of a long handle which allows impurities, such as froth, scum or fat, to be skimmed off oils, stocks and sauces. It is also very useful for removing cooked food from deep fryers as it is so light in weight the temperature of the oil is not lowered.

Slotted spoon Slotted spoons have long handles and perforations or slots which make it a handy utensil for removing or serving pieces of food that have been cooked in liquid, as the excess liquid drains through the holes in the spoon, keeping the food whole.

Soufflé dish A deep, straight-sided ovenproof dish used for sweet and savoury, hot and cold soufflés.

Spatula   Made from wood, plastic or rubber and used for scraping out bowls. Also a small and long implement with a bowl at one end used for handling small amounts of powder, eg. spices.

Strainer   A tool made from metal or other mesh which is used to separate solids out from liquids, eg. tea leaves and coffee grounds.

Tagine   A traditional Moroccan cooking pot, with a lid shaped like a tee-pee with a small hole in the top to allow the steam to escape. Vegetables, fish and meat

HANDY HINT

Straining fruit
Strain through a nylon sieve as wire ones taint or discolour the fruit.

are cooked in stews in the oven and then served from the dish.

Terrine dish   A heatproof earthenware dish with a lid, used for cooking terrines.

Timbale   A cup-shaped mould, traditionally lined with rice or pasta and filled with a creamy meat, fish or vegetable mixture. It also describes a light and creamy puréed mixture, which is baked in the mould, turned out and served with a sauce.

Tomato slicer   The stainless steel wires on these slicers are useful for cutting up tomatoes quickly and cleanly.

Tongs   Flexible U-shaped tool with long handles made from wood or metal used for removing or turning food on a barbeque, or from a hot pan or dish, with safety.

Waffle iron   Two oblong or round metal trays joined by a hinge with handles on opposite sides. The grooved surfaces of the trays give the waffles their characteristic square pattern. Instructions must be followed closely.

Wok   A Chinese pan with shallow, sloping sides, used mainly for stir-frying vegetables and noodles.

Zester   A tool for removing thin strips of surface peel, the zest, from citrus fruit. The strips of zest are used for flavouring and/or decoration.

Methods

Methods

Baking Cooking food by dry heat, generally in an oven.

Baking blind Cooking an empty pastry case, normally lined with parchment paper and filled with dried beans to keep the base flat and the sides upright.

Barding Covering lean meat, poultry and game with thin slices of pork fat or bacon to prevent the flesh from drying out during cooking.

Basting Moistening meat or poultry with pan juices during roasting by using a spoon or a bulb roaster.

Beating Mixing food to incorporate air, thus making it lighter and fluffier, with a spoon, a fork, a whisk or an electric beater.

Binding Adding cream, eggs, melted fat or water to a dry mixture to hold it together.

Blanching Plunging food briefly into boiling water to either set the colour of vegetables, or to loosen skin from, eg. nuts or tomatoes, or to remove bitter strong flavours.

Blending Combining ingredients with a spoon, an electric whisk or an electric blender to achieve a uniform mixture.

Boiling Cooking in liquid at a temperature of 100°C (212°F).

Boning Removing the bones from meat or poultry before rolling and/or stuffing.

Bottling Putting preserves or other foods into glass jars and sealing the jars under sterile conditions.

Braising Browning in hot fat and then slowly cooking in a covered pot with vegetables and a little liquid.

Brining	Immersing food in a strong salt and water solution.
Broiling	An American term for grilling.
Browning	Searing the outer surface of meat to seal in the juices and give a good colour to the gravy.
Candying	Cooking pieces of fruit or peel with sugar syrup to coat and preserve the food.
Caramelising	Changing sugar or mixtures with a high sugar content into caramel by applying heat until the substance turns brown.
Carving	Cutting slices of flesh from cooked meat or poultry with a sharp carving knife. It is advisable to leave the meat to stand for ten to fifteen minutes after removing from the heat source to allow the flesh to relax. This makes the task of carving easier and prevents the slices from falling apart.
Casseroling	Cooking a selection of vegetables, meat or poultry with water in a dish with a tight-fitting lid. The cooked food is normally served straight from the dish.
Chilling	Cooling food, without freezing it, in the refrigerator.
Chining	Separating the back bone from the ribs in a joint of meat to make carving easier.
Chopping	Cutting up food into varying different sizes with the aid of a sharp kitchen knife and a chopping board.
Churning	Agitating cream or milk in order to separate the oily globules from the watery whey to produce butter.
Clarifying	Removing sediments and impurities from certain foods, eg. fats such as butter and dripping can be cleared by heating and filtering. Consommé and jellies are cleared with beaten egg whites. Butter is clarified by melting it very gently over heat, removing the scum from the surface, then carefully filtering off the butter leaving the milky deposit in the bottom of the pan.
Clouturing	Studding meat or poultry with small pieces of barding fat, truffle, vegetables or other ingredient.
Coagulating	Congealing or thickening, as applied to fats when cooling or eggs when cooking.
Coating	Covering foods with a sauce or melted butter, or covering cooked or uncooked food with batter, egg or

breadcrumbs. When referring to the thickness of a sauce, such as custard, the sauce is cooked when it is thick enough to coat the back of a wooden spoon.

Coddling   Cooking eggs slowly in water below boiling point to a soft-boiled consistency.

Colloping   Cutting meat or vegetables into small pieces.

Concassing   A French term for roughly or finely chopping vegetables, most often used for tomatoes.

Coring   Removing the centre from fruit or vegetables without damaging the flesh. If the fruit or vegetable is cut into segments, the core can easily be cut away.

Creaming   Beating an ingredient or ingredients until the consistency of whipped cream is achieved, eg. butter and sugar in making a cake.

Crimping   Making a decorative border to the pastry of pies by pinching, or pressing with the thumb, the edges at regular intervals to give a fluted effect. Also applied to making deep cuts into fresh skate, then soaking in cold water and vinegar before cooking so that the flesh firms.

Cubing   Cutting any food into small square pieces, resembling dice.

Curdling   Causing fresh milk or a sauce to separate into solids and liquids by over-heating or by adding acid. The term also applies to cake mixtures that have separated when the eggs have been added too rapidly to creamed butter and sugar.

Curing   Treating meat, poultry, game or fish by salting, smoking or drying in order to preserve them. The curing process may be mild or strong.

Cutting in   Adding butter, fat or margarine to dry ingredients, chopping into small pieces with a knife and stirring until all the pieces are coated with the dry ingredients.

Daubing   Making incisions in meat and inserting strips of bacon in order to add flavour and moisture.

Decanting   Pouring liquid from one container into another, usually to remove unwanted matter such as sediment.

Decoting   Boiling a solution down to a concentrated liquid or essence.

Deep-frying   Frying in fat or oil where the items being cooked are completely immersed. When the right temperature has been reached any bubbling should cease and a slight haze rises from the surface. You can test the right temperature by dropping in a cube of bread which should then rise to the surface and brown rapidly. The deep-frying pan should only be half filled with fat as when the ingredients are added the fat will bubble up.

Deglazing   Removing browned meat from a pan, pouring off the fat and then adding a little liquid to the coagulated meat juices. With stirring and scraping this dissolves the sediment collected at the bottom of the pan, and the liquid is then gently heated to produce a concentrated extract which forms the basis of rich brown sauces.

Degorging   Extracting juices from meat, fish and vegetables by salting. This method is primarily used to remove indigestible or bitter juices.

Dehydrating/dessicating/drying Removing moisture from foodstuffs resulting in long-lasting products which may then be rehydrated with water. Examples include instant coffee, dried pulses and dried milk products.

Deseeding   Removing the pips or seeds from, eg. tomatoes or cucumbers.

Desiccating   See *dehydrating*.

Dicing   Cutting food into small cubes.

Diluting	Adding one liquid to another, eg. water to vinegar, thereby reducing the concentration.
Disjointing	Cutting poultry into pieces at the joints.
Dissolving	Mixing a dry ingredient with a liquid until it is totally absorbed into a liquid form. Often heat is used to aid this process.
Distilling	Heating a liquid so that it changes into a gas, and condensing by cooling. The different constituents will separate out at different rates so can be collected, eg. alcohol.
Draining	Drawing off liquid with the aid of a sieve or absorbent paper.
Drawing	Removing the entrails of poultry or game birds.
Dredging	Sprinkling or dusting with flour or sugar using a perforated dredger or a sieve.
Dressing	Garnishing a dish, or adding a dressing to a salad. The term is also used for plucking, drawing and trussing poultry and game.
Dry-frying	Frying food in a frying pan without the addition of fat or oil. Non-stick pans require no fat and are therefore ideal for this method of cooking.
Drying	See *dehydrating*.
Dusting	Sprinkling food lightly with another ingredient such as sugar or ground nuts.
Effervescing	Foaming or fermenting ingredients by activating a live ingredient, eg. yeast and sugar in water.
Egging	Coating food with raw beaten egg.
Farcing	Stuffing meat or poultry with a savoury mixture.
Fast freezing	Freezing food rapidly to avoid the formation of large ice crystals, which allow the loss of natural juices and flavour.
Filleting	Cutting the flesh from meat, poultry or fish away from the bone.
Filtering	Separating a liquid from a solid by straining through very fine muslin or a filter paper.
Flaking	Breaking up cooked fish into smaller pieces with a fork.
Fluting	See *crimping*.

Folding in	Adding one mixture to another by gently working them together with a metal spoon.
Fortifying	Adding flavour to an ingredient by enriching it with butter, eggs, cream or alcohol.
Frosting	A North American term for icing a cake.
Frothing	Dredging the surface of roast meat with flour and heating in a hot oven until it turns brown.
Frying	Cooking an ingredient in hot fat or oil.
Gelling	Reaching the consistency of jelly by setting.
Glazing	Giving sweet or savoury foods a glossy appearance by coating them with beaten egg, egg whites, milk or syrup.
Grating	Shredding solid foods by rubbing against a grater which has different-sized sharp perforations, to give varied grades of grated material, eg. finely-grated Parmesan, coarsely-grated Cheddar.
Greasing	Coating a cake tin, casserole, dish or baking tray with fat, butter or margarine to minimise sticking of the cooked food to the surface of the container.
Grilling	Cooking food quickly under radiant heat. Food for grilling should not exceed one inch or two and a half centimetres in thickness.
Grinding	Pounding or breaking down dry foods such as coffee beans, nuts or spices into a powder by means of a pestle and mortar, or in an electric grinder.
Gutting	Cleaning a fish by removing its intestines.
Hanging	Leaving meat or game suspended in a cool dry place for a few days to allow the air to circulate around it. This tenderises the flesh and develops the flavour.
Hard-boiling	Cooking an egg in its shell in boiling water until both the white and the yolk are set.

Hashing   Chopping or cutting food into small pieces.

Heating through Making cold cooked food thoroughly hot without boiling.

Hulling   Removing the calyx from soft fruits.

Infusing   Transferring flavour to a liquid by leaving the flavouring ingredient in for a period of time.

Jugging   Cooking in a heavy earthenware casserole or, as they did in times gone by, in a heavy lidded jug, eg. jugged hare.

Kneading   Working any dough or pastry to the correct consistency with the hands or with the dough hook attachment of a mixer.

Knocking back Kneading any yeasted mixture lightly after it has risen once and before it is moulded into specific shapes.

Knocking up   Making a decorative feature of the edges of sealed pastry pies by pressing the back of a knife into the edges to make horizontal lines. This raises the edges slightly.

Lacing   Adding of alcohol or assorted condiments or spices to a soup, sauce or stew.

Larding   Preparing meat for cooking by covering or inserting with pork fat or bacon to prevent drying out.

Liaising   Using a thickener such as cornflour, flour, arrowroot, potato flour or a mixture of cream and eggs in soups, sauces and stews.

Lining   Covering the inside of a cake tin or baking tray with parchment paper, foil or cling film to prevent sticking, or for easy removal after cooking or setting. It can also mean covering the inside of baking dishes with strips of bacon before filling with a mousse or pate.

Liquidising   Puréeing fruits and vegetables by hand through a sieve, or in an electric blender.

Macerating   Softening and flavouring foods by soaking in a liquid.

Marinating   Impregnating food with flavour and/or making it tender by immersing in a

	liquid containing a mixture of ingredients before cooking. The mixture is known as a marinade.
Mashing	Breaking down cooked food into very small particles for a purée with a fork or special masher.
Masking	Covering food with a thin layer of, eg. cream, sauce, icing.
Milling	See *grinding*.
Mincing	Cutting or chopping food, usually meat, into very small pieces, usually with the aid of a mincing machine or food processor.
Mortifier	To hang meat, poultry or game.
Mulling	Heating wine or beer with or without spices and sugar.
Napper	To coat or mask.
Paner	To egg and crumb any food before frying
Parboiling	Partially cooking foods in boiling water.
Paring	Thinly peeling vegetables or fruit.
Pasteurising	Treating milk with heat to destroy any potentially dangerous micro-organisms, without impairing the flavour.
Paunching	Removing the stomach and intestines of a rabbit or hare.
Peeling	Removing the skin from fruit or vegetables with a special instrument called a peeler.
Peppering	Sprinkling, seasoning or covering with crushed or ground peppercorns.
Pickling	Preserving foods by covering them in brine or vinegar in jars with the addition of spices, sugar and salt, and sealing the jars.
Piping	Decorating a dish with, eg. cream, icing, mashed potato or meringue, applied with a nozzle fitted to a fabric or paper bag.
Pipping	Removing seeds or pips from fruit or vegetables
Pitting	Removing stones from fruits, olives and dates. Also known as stoning.

Plucking	Removing feathers from poultry or game birds.
Poaching	Cooking by placing delicate foods, such as eggs and fish, in a gently simmering liquid until cooked.

Podding	Removing beans or peas from their outer casing, which is more commonly called a pod. Also known as shelling.
Pot-roasting	Cooking a tougher cut of meat slowly, by placing in a tightly-lidded dish with some liquid and vegetables and heating in the oven.
Potting	Putting puréed mixtures of meat, fish or poultry into small pots and sealing them by covering the top with a layer of melted fat.
Pounding	Tenderising meats by beating with a rolling pin or mallet which breaks down the fibres. It also refers to breaking down foods in a pestle and mortar.
Pre-cooking	Cooking one or more ingredients in advance to be used for future re-heating in another dish.
Preserving	Canning, bottling, deep freezing or otherwise treating perishable foods to extend their shelf life.
Pressing	Weighing down foods with very heavy weights so that they retain a neat shape when cold. It is also a method used for squeezing out juice from fruit or vegetables.
Proving	Leaving a yeast mixture to rise.
Puréeing	Pounding, sieving or liquidising fruit, vegetables, meat or fish to a smooth pulp.
Rasping	Making crumbs from dry bread.
Reconstituting	Adding liquid to a dried food to restore it to its original state.
Reducing	Boiling a liquid down until it is reduced in quantity and more concentrated in flavour.
Refreshing	Running cold water over just-cooked boiled vegetables or immersing in cold water to arrest cooking and set the colour.

Rendering	Cooking pieces of fat until they turn from solid pieces into a liquid.
Renvenir	To fry meat or vegetables quickly in hot fat in order to warm them through.
Resting	Setting aside of pastry to allow the gluten to develop the elasticity thereby lessening the chance of shrinkage during cooking. Also used for letting roast meat joints stand before carving.
Ripening	Allowing food to reach maturity.
Roasting	Cooking by dry heat, usually in the oven, using either fat from the food or additional fat to give the food a browned appearance.
Rolling out	Evenly flattening pastry or dough with a rolling pin or similar utensil.
Rubbing in	Incorporating fat into flour, by rubbing small pieces of fat between heavily floured fingers and thumbs until the mixture resembles fine breadcrumbs. This is often done now using a food processor.
Salting	Preserving food in dry salt or brine.
Sautéeing	Cooking with a small amount of fat, usually in a sauté pan, to lightly and quickly brown the food.
Scalding	Bringing a liquid, normally milk, up to a temperature just below boiling point. Also used for pouring boiling water over food to clean it, or to facilitate the removal of skin or hairs.
Scalloping	Decorating the double edge of a pastry pie by making small horizontal cuts and pulling and/or pushing the pastry with the back of a knife to achieve a scalloped effect.
Scoring	Cutting narrow parallel lines in food to improve the appearance and cook it more quickly.
Scrambling	Cooking beaten eggs over a gentle heat stirring constantly until they have reached a thickened creamy consistency.
Sealing	Braising the surface of meat, game or poultry in hot fat or in a hot oven to give good colour.
Searing	Sealing the surface of a food, usually meat, by browning quickly in a little very hot fat.

Seasoning	Enhancing the flavour of a dish by the addition of salt, pepper, herbs, spices, alcohol, lemon juice, etc.
Seething	See *simmering.*
Separating	Dividing one part of a substance from another, eg. removing the white of a raw egg from the yolk.
Setting	Reaching of the desired consistency, eg. firming of mousses, freezing of ice-creams, setting of jam.
Shallow-frying	Frying food with a small amount of fat in a shallow pan.
Shelling	Removing beans or peas from their outer casing, which is more commonly called a pod. Also known as podding.
Shredding	Cutting or grating food, usually vegetables, into very thin strips.
Sieving	Pushing foods, usually cooked, through a sieve to form a purée.
Sifting	Shaking dry food, eg. flour, through a mesh sieve to remove lumps and to incorporate air.
Simmering	Keeping a liquid bubbling gently just below boiling point.
Singeing	Using a flame to remove any residual feathers on plucked birds.
Skewering	Threading cubes of meat, fish or vegetables onto a metal or wooden spike prior to cooking
Skimming	Removing and discarding the froth from the surface of sauces, casseroles and jam. Either a skimmer, a spoon or absorbent kitchen paper may be used.
Skinning	Removing the skin of poultry, fish, fruit or vegetables.
Slaking	Mixing a starch with liquid, eg. cornflour with water, before adding it to a hot liquid for thickening purposes.
Smoking	Curing food by exposure to wood smoke.
Soaking	Covering with a liquid and leaving for a period.

HANDY HINT

Skinning peppers
Char under a hot grill until the skin blisters and turns black, place in a plastic bag to steam and when cooled remove skins easily.

Soft-boiling	Boiling an egg in its shell to the point where the white sets and the yolk remains soft.
Softening	Allowing fats to reach room temperature after being refrigerated. Also refers to tenderising by cooking.
Souring	Adding acid, usually lemon juice, to cream to give it a soured taste.
Sousing	Pickling in brine or vinegar. Often used for fish, particularly herring and mackerel.
Spit-roasting	Cooking on a rotating spit either over an open fire or in a cooker.
Standing	Allowing a joint of meat to rest before carving. Also used as a term in microwave cooking for leaving the dish in the microwave for a few minutes after cooking to allow the residual heat to spread evenly.
Steaming	Cooking food in the steam from boiling water.
Steeping	Covering food with hot or cold water and leaving it to stand, either to soften the food or to extract colour and/or flavour.
Sterilising	Destroying bacteria in food by heating to a high temperature.
Stewing	Simmering foods slowly for a long time in a container with a close-fitting lid to minimise evaporation.
Stir-frying	A quick method of frying. The food must be cut into small pieces and moved around the pan constantly until cooked.
Stirring	Moving a mixture around the pan to prevent burning or sticking, and eliminating the formation of lumps in a liquid to ensure a smooth well-blended sauce.
Stoning	Removing stones from fruits, olives and dates. Also known as pitting.
Straining	Draining the cooking liquor from the food, or separating solids from liquids, eg. in a soup.
Studding	Adding decorative and flavour-enhancing foods to a dish, eg. cloves to a gammon joint.

HANDY HINT

Skinning tomatoes
When skinning plunge into boiling water for 8 secs, run under the cold tap and the skins should come off a treat.

117

Stuffing	Filling the cavities of foods with a mixture of ingredients, usually savoury.
Sweating	Cooking sliced or diced vegetables slowly in fat with a lid on the pan to produce steam and thus prevent browning.
Swirling	Adding one liquid to another to produce a rippled effect, eg. sour cream stirred into beetroot soup.
Tempering	Heating chocolate with a high cocoa content to melting point and rapidly cooling it by working it with a palette knife on a marble slab. Used when making chocolate products, or decorating with chocolate.
Tenderising	Beating raw meat with a wooden mallet or other heavy implement to break down the fibres and make it more tender when cooked.
Thickening	See *liaising*.
Toasting	Browning food, usually bread, under a grill.
Topping and tailing	Removing the stem and bottom end of fruit or vegetables, eg. gooseberries, French beans.
Tossing	Turning foods over in a dish to ensure an even coating of butter or dressing. It also applies to the flipping over of pancakes to ensure both sides are cooked.
Trussing	Tying or skewering poultry and game birds into neat shapes before cooking.
Warming up	Heating a pre-cooked dish slowly to below boiling point.
Whipping	Whisking liquid ingredients to incorporate air and/or to thicken.
Whisking	Aerating and/or combining mixtures.
Working	Moulding a soft mixture into shapes or drawing a crumbly mixture together to form a smooth pastry or dough.

Sundries

Breads and yeasted goods

Bagel A Jewish speciality, these ring-shaped rolls are boiled before baking and come in different flavours, sweet and savoury.

Bap These white breakfast rolls originated in Scotland and are best eaten straight from the oven, split and spread with butter. They are heavily dusted with flour.

Bara brith A Welsh yeasted loaf heavily laden with fruit.

Barrel bread A cylindrical loaf baked in a ridged tin. The ridges leave indentations on the loaf which make it easier to slice evenly.

Batch loaf Popular in Scotland, these loaves are baked close together so that the dough touches and are split apart after baking to reveal soft sides with crusty tops and bottoms.

Bath bun Dating back to the eighteenth century, these buns are made from a white yeasted dough containing mixed peel, sugar and sultanas. The mixture is placed in spoonfuls on the baking tray, brushed with egg and sprinkled with crushed sugar cubes before baking.

Black bread A generic name for various dark and heavy Continental breads made from rye and wholewheat flours.

Bloomer loaf Usually made with white flour with the top characterised by six diagonal slashes, this nine inch long loaf is tapered at the end.

Boston brown bread This heavy steamed bread originated in North America, and is made from brown and white flours, polenta or semolina and treacle. It is traditionally eaten with Boston baked beans.

Bridge roll Originally served at bridge parties, these finger-length soft white rolls are generally split, filled and sandwiched back together again.

Brioche	This French, rich yeasted batter is made from milk, water, eggs and butter. It is light in texture with a golden crust, shaped and cooked in special fluted brioche moulds individually or in one large loaf. Brioche are best eaten warm with jam and butter or hollowed out and filled with sautéed mushrooms, or other savoury fillings.
Challah	Made from a yeasted dough containing eggs and shaped like a plait, this Jewish bread is traditionally served on the Sabbath.
Chapatti	Made from fine-ground wholewheat flour, this unleavened Indian speciality, which is cooked on a griddle or shallow-fried, is torn up and used to mop up curries.
Chelsea bun	These buns resemble pinwheels as the white yeasted dough is rolled out, brushed with egg, sprinkled with currants and sugar and rolled up like a Swiss roll, cut into slices and baked. Usually served at tea-time.
Ciabatta	An Italian flat oblong-shaped loaf made from flour, water and olive oil. Delicious hot with salads, soups and pasta dishes.
Cob	Made from white or brown flour, this round loaf is baked on a greased baking tray and sometimes is made with a criss-cross pattern on top.
Coburg loaf	A round loaf with a cross cut in the top.
Corn bread	This bread is popular in North America and is made from cornmeal, which is deep yellow in colour.
Cottage loaf	A white, round loaf with a knob on top.
Croissant	Another French breakfast speciality, made from a rich dough of flour, milk and butter in a similar way to puff pastry. These soft, crescent-shaped rolls are delicious with butter and jam or, as in France, with a strong cup of coffee.
Crumpet	My favourite! They are round, fairly flat and made from a yeasted batter and should be ideally toasted on a griddle, flat side first and then on the honeycomb side, spread with masses of butter and then eaten immediately. Be careful as the butter tends to drip through the holes.

Damper This unleavened bread hails from Australasia, where it is often baked in the ashes of a bonfire or barbecue.

Dark rye bread This Eastern European bread with its hard crust will last for at least a week when wrapped in foil and stored in a cool place. Ideally it is sliced very thinly and used to make open sandwiches with smoked meats, fish or cheese.

English muffin A favourite in America for brunch. They are pulled apart and toasted, topped with either sweet or savoury goodies.

Foccacia The oldest of Italian breads, it was traditionally baked on a hot stone in a wood-fired hearth. This bread is shaped in a round and either baked plain with salt and herbs or has other flavourings added.

French bread Probably the most common of foreign breads, it has a hard crust and is shaped into long sticks or baguettes. It only has a couple of hours shelf life when made in the authentic French style.

Germ bread White or wholemeal bread baked with added wheatgerm, usually sold under proprietary brand names.

Grissini Long, very thin sticks of bread baked until crisp. Italians like to eat these with drinks or accompanying a meal instead of bread.

Gugelhupf A speciality yeasted bread from Germany, Austria and Alsace, it resembles a spongy mixture containing flour, sugar, eggs, lemon peel, chopped almonds, raisins and milk. It is traditionally baked in a deep, fluted mould and iced when cold.

Hot cross bun These yeasted, fruited and spiced buns are traditionally eaten on Good Friday for breakfast. The cross on top made of pastry is supposed to represent the cross upon which Jesus died.

Johnny cake A North American cake made from maize meal.

Lardy cake This slightly sweet, flaky pastry cake based on lard is baked in a Yorkshire pudding mould and scored into diamonds.

Light rye bread This slightly sour bread is popular in the States where it is traditionally filled with salt beef , pastrami or ham.

Limpa bread A speciality from Sweden, this dark yeasted rye bread containing anise or crushed fennel, is slightly sweetened with the equivalent of black treacle.

HANDY HINT

To revive a stale loaf
Wrap in foil and bake in a hot oven for 5-10 minutes.

Linseed bread A German speciality bread made from wholewheat flour and the whole seeds of the linseed plant, very good for digestion and excellent with strong-tasting German sausages and cheeses.

Malt bread Malt extract, black treacle and mixed fruit are added to this plain white yeasted dough.

Matzo Another Jewish speciality unleavened bread, similar to water biscuits, eaten during Passover. They contain no salt.

Mohnkuchen This white yeasted dough filled and topped with a sweet rich mixture of poppy seeds, originates from Central Europe where it is dusted with icing sugar and served in pieces.

Muffin A North Country speciality made from rounds of yeasted dough cooked on a griddle or in the oven. Also known in the United States as cupcakes which are served either warm or cold.

Naan An tear-shaped, Indian, rich leavened bread traditionally baked in a tandori oven, slapped on the side of the clay.

Pain perdu/French toast Slices of bread which are dipped in a mixture of beaten eggs, milk and vanilla, fried until brown on both sides, then dusted with icing sugar before serving.

Pandoro A sweet, yeasted bread from Verona in Italy.

Paratha Delicious Indian unleavened bread, enriched with butter and shallow fried. It can be stuffed with either sweet or savoury fillings.

Pitta bread Flat, slightly leavened bread from the Middle East. Shaped in rounds or ovals, they are eaten hot and traditionally slit and filled with grilled lamb and salad. In Greece they are eaten plain, tearing off bits to scoop up local dips, such as houmous.

Poppadom   These large, round Indian crisps, made from lentil flour, are available plain or spicy and need only to be deep-fried or grilled for a short time. They should be eaten immediately with curries and traditional chutneys.

Pretzel   Savoury and biscuit-like, pretzels are usually crisp but the larger ones may be soft inside, and all are crusted with salt crystals and twisted into many shapes.

Pumpernickel/volkornbrot This bread is slightly lighter than the dark rye and has a much shorter shelf life as it loses its moisture quicker.

Puri   Deep-fried puffy chapatti.

Rum baba   This is made from a sweet, light, yeasted dough and baked in a special baba mould. The babas are then soaked in rum-flavoured syrup and decorated traditionally with whipped cream, glacé cherries and pieces of angelica.

Sally Lunn   This white yeast dough enriched with eggs and butter was named after the girl who supposedly sold this bread in Bath. After baking and glazing, it is split in half, filled with cream and eaten while still warm.

Savarin   A ring cake made from a sweet, yeasted white dough steeped in rum-flavoured syrup and glazed with apricot jam.

Scandinavian crispbread As rye is the most filling cereal grain these crispbreads are popular with slimmers. They are available in dark and light rye and can be sprinkled with sesame seeds.

Soda bread/Irish soda bread Bicarbonate of soda or buttermilk is used as a raising agent in this unyeasted brown or white bread traditionally from Ireland.

Sour dough   This bread dough, in which the yeast is still alive and active, is reserved from one baking to use as a leaven in the next. Used mainly in Scandinavia, Eastern Europe and North American.

Pasta

Pasta is made from hard durum wheat by mixing together flour and water to make the basic dough. Pasta fresca is fresh pasta with eggs added to the dough, and pasta verde has puréed spinach added to the dough.

TO COOK PASTA

Allow 50-75 gm (2-3 oz) per person. Place pasta into a large pan of boiling water. Bring back to the boil and allow to simmer uncovered until it is completely tender, yet still firm, stirring occasionally. Fresh pasta will be done in the time it takes for the water to return to a full boil. Pasta should not be over-cooked or under-cooked and can be tested by biting a strand. It should be 'al dente', literally 'to the tooth', ie. slightly firm to the bite. For dried pasta cook according to the instructions on the packet. Drain pasta in a colander, cover with a sauce of your choice and serve immediately.

The types of pasta listed below are a selection from the very many available. They have been grouped by shape rather than any other criteria. In the definitions any words in inverted commas are translations from Italian.

CYLINDRICAL

Fedelini 'Little faithful ones', these are very fine rods of spaghetti.

Lungo-vermicelli coupe Long vermicelli cut into pieces.

Spaghetti The word 'spaghetti' means 'little strings', and is more commonly known as vermicelli in Southern Italy.

Spaghettini This is a thinner version of spaghetti.

Vermicelli Very fine spaghetti.

Angel's hair   See *capellini.*

Bavettine   Narrow linguine.

Capelli d'angelo See *capellini.*

Capellini   Fine ribbon pasta lengths. Angel's hair is
the thinnest variety, also known as capelli
d'angelo.

Capelvenere   Fine ribbon noodles.

Cellophane noodles Transparent noodles, usually made from mung
bean starch paste, but they can also be made from pea
starch or wheat starch.

Egg noodles   The main difference between noodles and Italian pasta
is in the way they are prepared rather than the
ingredients. The darker yellow ones have more egg
added than the lighter ones. Egg noodles are normally
bought in varying sized bundles, and have usually been
pre-cooked by steaming so they require only a minimal
amount of preparation.

Fettucce   'Ribbons', this pasta is the widest of the fettuccine
family.

Fettuccine   Narrow ribbons of egg noodles.

Lasagne/lasagna This is the broadest of the ribbon pasta and can be
bought either smooth, ridged or with a ruffled edge.

Lasagnette   A smaller version of the ruffle-edged lasagne that is
about three quarters of an inch wide.

Linguine   'Little tongues', these are thick narrow ribbons of pasta.

Maccheroni alla chitarra These are ribbon noodles that have been cut
with the steel wires of a special guitar-like tool. They
are also called tonnarelli.

Malfalda   Broad ribbon noodles which are rippled on both sides
and are wider than fettucine.

Margherita   Named after Margherita daisies, these are narrow
ribbon noodles, rippled only on one side.

Pappardelle   Broad ribbon noodles, traditionally served with game
sauces.

Pizzoccheri   Thick dark buckwheat noodles.

Rice noodles   As the name suggests, these noodles are made from rice flour and are produced as long strands before being folded over into bundles.

Tagliarini   Similar to tagliatelli but smaller in width.

Tagliatelle   These flat quarter inch wide ribbon noodles are a speciality of Bologna.

Tonnarelli   See *maccheroni alla chitarra*.

Trenette   A narrower thicker version of tagliatelle.

TUBES

Bucatini   Short straight macaroni.

Coralli   Small pasta tubes for soup.

Ditali   'Finger of a glove' or 'thimble' are short macaroni.

Ditalini   Smaller version of ditali.

Elocoidali   A smaller version of rigatoni but with a spiral line pattern.

Macaroni/maccheroni This is the generic term for all types of pasta, but is more commonly used to describe the hollow wider version of spaghetti.

Magliette   'Links', this pasta is slightly curved, hollow and short in length.

Mezzane   Slightly curved macaroni that has been cut into short lengths.

Mostaccioli   See *penne*.

Occhi di lupo   Large tubes of pasta, 'wolf's eyes'.

Penne   Quill-shaped pasta, cut on the diagonal at both ends. It can be ribbed and is available in varying sizes.

Perciatelli   Long, thin hollow macaroni that looks like thick spaghetti.

Pipe rigate   A ridged pasta in the shape of a bent pipe.

Rigatoni   Large grooved macaroni.

Tubettilunghi   Similar to macaroni but with a slight bend. It is also known as elbow macaroni.

Ziti   'Bridegrooms', another version of slightly curved macaroni cut into short lengths.

Anelli   Small, round ring-shaped pasta.

Bozzoli   Named after its cocoon-like
                    shape.

Cappelli di pagliaccio Pasta shaped like a 'clown's hat'.

Casareccia   Pasta lengths that are curled into shape, with a twist at
                    one end.

Cavatappi   Ridged pasta in a twisted shape.

Cavatelli   Short crinkle-edged shells.

Conchiglie piccole rigate Small pasta sea shells.

Conchiglie rigate Pasta shaped like conch sea shells.

Cresti di gallo Similar shape to a cock's comb, made from ridged
                    pasta.

Diamanti   Pasta shaped into an elongated diamond.

Farfalle   Pasta shaped like a butterfly.

Farfallini   Small butterfly shapes.

Festonati   'Garland' or 'festoon', this pasta is about two inches
                    long with indentations down the middle.

Fiochetti   Pasta shaped like bows.

Fusilli   Pasta shaped like a spiral corkscrew.

Fusilli bucati Pasta shaped like small springs.

Gramigna   'Grass', these are small grass-like shapes, curled at the
                    ends.

Lancette   This pasta is shaped like 'little spears'.

Lingue di passero Pasta shaped like a 'sparrow's tongue'.

Lumache medie   Pasta shaped like 'snails'.

Maltagliati   Pasta cut into irregular shapes.

Maruzze   Literally, 'seashells'.

Occhi di passeri Tiny circles of pasta, 'sparrow's eyes'.

Orecciette   Pasta shaped like 'little ears'.

Orzo   Rice-shaped or barley-shaped pasta.

Pastina   The general term used for the wide variety of tiny pasta
                    shapes usually cooked in soups.

Quadrettini   Small flat squares of pasta.

Riccini   'Little curls' are a shell-like ridged pasta.

Rotelle	Pasta shaped like 'small wheels'.
Ruoti	This pasta is shaped like a spiked wheel.
Ruotini	A smaller version of ruoti.
Spirale	This pasta is twisted together to form a spiral and cut into short lengths.

DUMPLINGS AND STUFFED PASTA

Agnolotti	'Priest's caps', these are crescent-shaped meat-filled ravioli.
Cannelloni	Hollow cylindrical pasta which is stuffed and baked. Italian word for 'big pipes'.
Capelletti	Pasta with a circular hat shape, which is stuffed.
Gnocchi	Small dumplings made from durum wheat, potatoes or semolina.
Gnocchi sardi	A small version of gnocchi, thus named for their sardine shape.
Manicotti	'Muffs', these are giant tubes of pasta used for stuffing.
Ravioli	The best known of the pasta dumplings, it is square in shape and traditionally stuffed with spinach and ricotta, but can be also bought filled with a savoury meat filling.
Tortellini	According to legend, this small stuffed pasta dumpling was modelled on Venus's navel! Traditionally it can be stuffed with minced chicken breast, pork, mortadella or bologna sausage, cheese and nutmeg or spinach, and now other ingredients are often used.

Pastry

A paste-like mixture made from flour and water. A richer dough can be made with the addition of fat, milk, sugar and/or eggs. It is the way in which these ingredients are added and combined together that differentiates one pastry from another. With the exception of choux, all pastries are rolled out with a rolling pin. Here is a selection of some of the best.

American short crust American pastry has more of a shortbread texture than English short crust, because the fat is chopped and blended into the pastry rather than being rubbed in. More often vegetable fats are used rather than lard, so rubbing in by hand would render the pastry sticky.

Choux pastry/pâte choux This pastry contains plain flour, salt, water, butter and eggs. The flour is added to boiling water and butter, and the beaten eggs are added when the mixture has cooled. The final mixture can then be piped or spooned into whatever shape the dish requires. It is important to sift the flour to avoid lumps. The beating of the mixture should be just enough to bring the paste away from the pan, which indicates that the flour is cooked. Over-beating at this point will result in the pastry failing to rise properly and becoming cake-like in consistency. Beating very thoroughly is important when adding the eggs. When cooking choux, the oven should be hot, and under no circumstances should it be removed from the oven until it is firm to the touch, otherwise the pastry will fall immediately and become soggy.

Filo/fillo/phyllo Very thin pastry originating from the Balkans, similar to strudel. It is used for both sweet and savoury dishes.

Flaky pastry This is a combination of short crust and puff pastry methods. A portion of the fat is rubbed into the flour initially, with the addition of cold water to make a firm paste. The pastry is then rolled out with the remaining fat pressed onto it in small pieces: the paste is then folded and rolled out like puff pastry. The success of the pastry lies in the correct rolling out in cool conditions so as not to melt the fat, otherwise the pastry will tend to be greasy when cooked.

HANDY HINT

Pastry rolling
Roll out pastry between two sheets of cling film, this keeps the board clean and allows the pastry to be moved without cracking.

Hot-water crust This pastry is used for raised pies such as pork, veal and game. It is made by adding boiling water and lard to flour. The handling of the pastry once made should be carried out swiftly, for the paste must be moulded into shape before the lard has time to set and become brittle.

Pâte à paté A type of short crust suitable for French raised pies. It is made in the French fashion, as with pâte brisée.

Pâte à tartelettes This pastry, although similar to pâte sucrée, is more economical and slightly crisper because it does not contain eggs.

Pâte brisée This paste is similar to short crust but made in the French way, by sifting the flour on to a marble slab, making a depression in the middle, adding the salt, water, butter and egg and gradually working in the flour. It is used for either sweet or savoury dishes.

Pâte frollée This pastry contains pounded or ground almonds.

Pâte moulée Similar to pâte à paté but not quite so rich.

Pâte sucrée This crisp, short sweet pastry is not the easiest to make, but the secret lies in the careful blending of the ingredients and the lightness of handling. This pastry is made in the French way, with the addition of sugar, and is used widely for making tarts, flans and in all patisserie work. Either castor or icing sugar is used, but it is advisable to use castor sugar if lining large flans as the icing sugar may cause the pastry to spread. Try not to add more flour than the recipe allows as this will spoil the finished texture by making it tough.

Puff pastry This pastry is considered to be the finest of all the pastries, although it is probably the most complicated to make. Always use the best flour available and firm, slightly salted butter. The water used in the process should be ice cold with a squeeze of lemon juice to acidulate it. The flour and water should be made into a paste which should be firm enough to hold the butter pieces when added, but not too firm, which would make it difficult to roll. The flour and water should be mixed as quickly as possible to avoid any elasticity of the dough. A knob of butter the size of a walnut can be added into the flour initially to avoid this happening. The butter should be firm but not soft, as if it is the same consistency of the pastry it makes the rolling out process easier. Try to avoid adding too much flour when rolling out as this toughens the cooked pastry.

Rich short crust The same method as with short crust applies for this richer version but with the addition of either a beaten egg or egg yolk, and a higher proportion of fat to flour. This pastry is a better option if the dish is to be eaten cold. It is best to leave the pastry in the fridge for at least half an hour before rolling out to prevent the pastry from shrinking during cooking.

Rough puff Very similar to puff pastry, although it is simpler to make as the proportion of butter to flour is not so high. It appears flakier and generally has no lard in it.

Short crust The most versatile of all pastries, used for flans, tarts, and fruit and savoury pies. Plain flour is used and a proportion of half fat to flour. The fat is cut into small pieces or grated into the flour and rubbed in as fast as possible until the mixture resembles fine breadcrumbs. Water is used for mixing, although if a softer pastry is required milk may be added in its place. As with rich short crust the pastry should be chilled for at least half an hour before rolling out.

Strudel pastry This pastry originates from Hungary, where the finest of white flour can be found, giving the finished product its characteristic wafer-like crispness. Used in all sweet and savoury strudels.

Suet crust Self-raising flour, or plain flour with baking powder added, can be used together with chopped or shredded suet to make a light fluffy pastry, with two-thirds flour to one-third suet. Water or milk is added to bind the dough, the consistency of which should be similar to a light scone mixture. It is traditionally used for steak and kidney pudding.

HANDY HINTS

Extra light pastry
Add a little lemon juice
to the chilled water.

Avoid stretching pastry when rolling out
If pastry is stretched during handling this will result in shrinkage during baking.

Rest pastry for 30 mins
This makes the pastry easier to handle, including rolling out.

Sauces

Aillade   A French mayonnaise flavoured with garlic and walnuts.

Aioli sauce   Based on mayonnaise, this sauce is highly flavoured with crushed garlic. An alternative version can be made with breadcrumbs, milk, garlic, egg yolks, olive oil and lemon juice.

Allemande   A suprême sauce with egg yolks and cream added.

Anchovy essence   Used to enhance savoury dishes, this pink salty sauce made from anchovies should be used sparingly. When mixed with soy sauce, it is a useful substitute for fish sauce in Asian cooking.

Andalouse   Tomato purée is added to mayonnaise together with finely chopped pimentos.

Angostura bitters   This pink, clove-scented liquid, containing quinine and spices, was originally created as a remedy for fever. It enhances the flavour of mustard and tarragon sauces, and can also be added to dishes such as shepherd's pie, beef stew or baked beans. More commonly found in the bar, it adds flavour to drinks such as champagne cocktails and pink gins!

Apple sauce   Purée made from apples, sugar, butter and lemon juice used to accompany roast pork.

Aurore sauce   Tomato purée and fish stock are the main ingredients of this velouté sauce.

Avgolemono sauce   A Greek white coating sauce made with lemon and egg.

Bagna cauda   Chopped anchovies, garlic and basil are added to melted butter and oil. This Italian speciality is served hot as a dip for raw or cooked vegetables.

Béarnaise sauce A thickened mixture of egg yolks, fresh tarragon, shallots and vinegar.

Béchamel sauce This classic French white sauce is made with milk infused with bay leaves, parsley, cloves, nutmeg, peppercorns and onion.

Beurre blanc Another classic French sauce made from a concentrated mixture of white wine, vinegar and shallots into which small pieces of butter are slowly added. The sauce is beaten over a low heat until it is thick enough to coat the back of a spoon.

Beurre composé This well-creamed butter may be made with the addition of a variety of ingredients to complement the food being served. For example, parsley butter is served with cod. The finished butter is formed into a sausage shape and refrigerated until firm. Slices about a quarter inch thick are then placed on the hot food.

Bigarade An espagnole sauce flavoured with orange.

Black butter sauce Clarified butter is heated slowly until it turns a deep brown, and it is then flavoured with vinegar and chopped capers.

Bolognaise sauce A thick meat and tomato sauce traditionally served with pasta.

Bordelaise sauce An espagnole sauce flavoured with shallots, thyme, tarragon, red wine, lemon juice and parsley.

Bread sauce Thick sauce made from white bread, onions, butter and milk, flavoured with cloves, bay and pepper. Excellent with roast chicken and turkey.

Brown sauce A combination of water, malt vinegar, cane molasses, sugar, rye flour, spices, onions, tomatoes, dates, tamarind and soy sauce makes this favourite British sauce. Also used to describe the classic brown sauce which forms the basis for many other sauces.

Caboul sauce A mayonnaise flavoured with curry powder.

Chantilly mayonnaise Whipped cream is added to mayonnaise.

Chasseur sauce An espagnole sauce flavoured with extra onions, fried mushrooms and tomato purée.

HANDY HINT

Prevention of skin forming on sauces Cover with cling film.

135

Chaudfroid Made from equal amounts of hot béchamel sauce and cold liquid aspic jelly, this sauce is used to coat fish, chicken and turkey for cold buffets.

Chilli sauce A combination of red chilli peppers, spices and tomatoes makes up this spicy sauce, which can range from mild to very hot.

Choron sauce Béarnaise sauce is flavoured with tomato purée to give a pinkish colour.

Cranberry sauce Port and oranges are sometimes added to this sauce, made from cranberries, which traditionally accompanies roast turkey.

Crème à l'anglaise The French word for custard.

Cumberland sauce The cold version is made from red wine flavoured with orange, lemon, redcurrant jelly, onion, spices and seasoning. The mixture is heated, strained and cooled. The hot sauce is made from a basis of port thickened with cornflour and flavoured with orange, lemon, herbs and redcurrant jelly.

Custard A sauce made from eggs, milk, vanilla and sugar. It can be served warm or cold with desserts and puddings.

Demi-glace sauce An espagnole sauce, flavoured with meat juices and dry sherry, and reduced by boiling until glossy and thick enough to coat the back of a spoon.

Diane sauce A poivrade sauce enriched with cream and excellent with steaks.

Doria sauce A béchamel sauce flavoured with chopped cooked cucumber and a hint of nutmeg.

Dutch sauce A béchamel sauce flavoured with lemon juice and thickened with egg yolk and cream.

Duxelle sauce Finely-chopped mushrooms and shallots are sweated with butter and/or white wine and added to a velouté sauce.

Epicurienne sauce Mayonnaise flavoured with chopped gherkins and chutney.

Espagnole sauce A classic French brown sauce made from sautéed root vegetables, flour, fat, tomato purée, fresh tomatoes and meat stock.

HANDY HINT

Lumpy sauces
Correct by straining, whisking or putting in a blender.

Estragon sauce A velouté sauce made with fish stock and flavoured with tarragon.

Fish sauce Small fish, such as anchovies, are fermented in barrels under the midday sun for several months, resulting in a horrible-smelling, salty brown liquid, which is used predominantly in South East Asian cooking. In Thailand it is called *nam pla*, and in Vietnam and Laos *nuoc mam*. Despite its smell, it is delicious, especially when mixed with garlic, lime juice, sugar and chilli to make a dipping sauce for fried foods and dumplings.

French dressing A classic salad dressing made from oil, salt, vinegar, mustard powder and pepper.

Fruit sauce This sauce contains tomatoes, vinegar and raisins, and is similar to tomato ketchup but darker in colour.

Gravy A traditional British sauce made from meat juices, flour and vegetable water or stock.

Gribiche sauce Similar to mayonnaise, this French sauce is made from mashed hard-boiled egg yolks blended with oil, vinegar and/or lemon juice. It is then flavoured with chopped capers, herbs and gherkins. Thin strips of egg white are added last of all.

Hard sauce North American word for brandy butter and rum butter.

Harissa sauce A North African chilli sauce used as a condiment.

Harvey sauce This sauce includes anchovies, garlic, cayenne, soy and vinegar. It resembles a relish and is used in the same way as Worcester sauce.

Hoisin sauce This anise-flavoured sauce is soya bean-based, with the addition of chillies, garlic and several spices, and varies in thickness. Commonly known for its part in Peking duck, the sweet and spicy, red-brown sauce is used to coat the pancake before the cucumber, spring onions and shredded duck are added. Pure heaven!

Hollandaise sauce A classic French sauce made from egg yolks emulsified with butter, vinegar and/or lemon juice in a double saucepan. It is custard-like in consistency and is served with meat, fish and vegetables.

HANDY HINT

Hollandaise curdling
Caused by overheating, add an ice cube to cool the mixture down and it will reform.

Horseradish sauce Horseradish relish is combined with crème fraiche or cream to give a creamier and milder accompaniment to meats and fish.

Hungarian sauce A velouté sauce made with fish, poultry or meat stock with the addition of lightly fried onions and paprika.

Kecap manis Indonesian soy sauce.

Ketchup A spicy sauce or condiment, the best-known of which is tomato. Ketchup was very popular in Victorian times and was more commonly made from oysters, lobsters and eels, all of which were cheap foods then. Ketchup is used to enliven bland foods, and is best when home-made but nowadays time is limited and it is generally bought ready-prepared. Walnut ketchup and mushroom ketchup are both good when used in dark, robust sauces or steak and kidney pie.

Lyonnaise sauce An espagnol sauce which is flavoured with fried onions.

Maltaise sauce This is a hollandaise sauce with the addition of grated orange rind and strained orange juice from blood oranges.

Marie Rose sauce Mayonnaise with the addition of tomato ketchup, this goes well with prawns.

Mayonnaise An emulsion of eggs, oil and vinegar or lemon juice. This sauce forms the basis of countless other sauces, eg. with anchovy essence it becomes a rémoulade.

Melba sauce This sauce was named after Dame Nellie Melba, and is made from puréed and sieved raspberries and lemon juice, slightly thickened with icing sugar.

Mint sauce/mint jelly A blend of sweetened fresh mint and vinegar, traditionally served with lamb. Mint jelly is made from apple jelly with the addition of mint. It is also served with lamb, and is sweeter and less pungent than mint sauce.

Mole sauce A Mexican sauce made from chillies, onions, garlic, tomatoes, raisins, tortillas and chocolate. Sometimes almonds or sesame seeds are added.

Mornay sauce A béchamel sauce flavoured with cheese, usually gruyère, parmesan or cheddar, and mustard.

Mousseline sauce Softly whipped cream is added to hollandaise.

Mustard sauce Based on hollandaise but with the addition of mustard and peppercorns. The type of mustard is a matter of choice.

Neapolitan sauce An Italian tomato sauce flavoured with onion, basil and parsley.

Newburg sauce A cream sauce made with sherry, flavoured with onions and thickened with egg yolks. It is traditionally served with lobster.

Onion sauce White sauce with added sliced boiled onions, flavoured with cloves, used to accompany roast lamb.

Oxford sauce A cold sauce, similar to Cumberland sauce, made by heating port, redcurrant jelly, orange and lemon juice, spices and seasoning and allowing to cool.

Oyster sauce A thick brown sauce popular in Chinese cookery made with oysters cooked in soy sauce and brine.

Panada A white sauce twice the thickness of a coating sauce is made from a roux of fat and flour. It is used as a binding ingredient, eg. for croquettes and souffles.

Parsley sauce White sauce with added chopped parsley. Delicious with boiled ham and broad beans.

Pesto sauce Chopped basil, crushed garlic, pinenuts and parmesan cheese are the main ingredients of this Italian sauce which complements pasta beautifully.

Piri piri A hot condiment, similar to tabasco, which originated in the old Portuguese colonies in Africa.

Plum sauce Dark red plums are preserved with chilli, ginger, vinegar, sugar and spices to make this thick sweet and sour Chinese sauce.

Poivrade sauce Sauce made with vegetables, stock and wine vinegar, with crushed peppercorns added at the end of cooking.

Portugaise sauce This is similar to espagnole sauce but contains more fresh tomatoes.

Pouring sauce The usual proportion for this sauce is fifteen grams or half an ounce thickening agent to half a pint of milk or other liquid.

Ravigote dressing Fresh tarragon, chervil, parsley, chopped capers, chopped hard-boiled egg, onion and French mustard are added to a velouté sauce.

Rémoulade sauce Mayonnaise flavoured with chopped anchovies or anchovy essence, French mustard, chopped gherkins, chopped capers and chopped fresh herbs.

Robert sauce An espagnole sauce flavoured with dry white wine and French mustard.

Roux A French word for a mixture of equal amounts of melted fat and flour used to thicken sauces.

Sabayon sauce A French sauce containing egg yolks, sugar, sherry and water. Sometimes whipped cream is folded in and served with fruit desserts.

Salad cream Sharper in flavour than mayonnaise, liquid rather than solid and not so rich.

Salsa verde Vinaigrette flavoured with crushed garlic, chopped anchovies, chopped parsley and capers.

Sambal Similar to a chutney made with a variety of fruit and vegetables, this spicy accompaniment is commonly used in Oriental and Indian cooking.

Sauce verte A mayonnaise flavoured with fresh chopped parsley, chervil, tarragon, watercress and chives.

Shrimp paste Made from dried, salted, fermented shrimp, this Malaysian paste, known as 'blachan', is used in stir-fries.

Smitane sauce A velouté sauce made with poultry or game stock, and flavoured with shallots, vinegar, sour cream and white wine.

Soubise sauce A béchamel sauce flavoured with boiled puréed onions, nutmeg and cream.

Soy sauce Defatted soya bean pulp and wheat or barley flour are fermented to produce this dark sauce. Good soy sauce has a rich aroma and is salty and pungent. It heightens the flavour of dishes and is used in Oriental cooking in place of salt.

Spanish sauce See *espagnole sauce*.

Suprême sauce Velouté sauce made from chicken stock with added cream and butter.

Sweet and sour sauce This sauce is a mixture of soy sauce, vinegar and sugar and is used in Oriental cuisine.

Tabasco sauce Named after the region where the red chilli peppers originate in Mexico, this sauce is a mixture of these fiery peppers and vinegar.

Tahina/tahini A paste made from toasted ground sesame seeds, widely used in the Middle East in Latin America, and is an important ingredient in houmous. Tahina can itself be drizzled with olive oil, garnished with black olives and chopped parsley and eaten as an appetiser.

Tartare sauce Mayonnaise made with hard-boiled egg yolks with the addition of capers, lemon juice and parsley.

Thousand Island dressing Green peppers and chilli sauce are added to mayonnaise to create this sauce.

Tomato sauce Classic sauce made from tomatoes, onion, carrot, garlic, flour, sugar, seasonings and stock.

Velouté sauce Similar to a béchamel sauce except stock is used rather than milk. It can sometimes have cream and lemon added.

Wasabi This is a Japanese horseradish, unrelated to the European horseradish, and a member of the cabbage family. Most commonly used in sushimi, either coarsely ground or powdered, to give this dish a kick. It can be mixed with water to give the paste that we know, but use sparingly so as not to blow your head off!

White butter sauce See *beurre blanc*.

White sauce This is similar to béchamel but unflavoured milk is used.

Worcestershire sauce This hot and spicy sauce contains molasses, sugar, garlic, anchovies, garlic, seasoning and tamarind. It is used in many meat dishes and marinades, and is an ingredient in the vodka-based drink Bloody Mary.

Zabaglione sauce A light-textured Italian sweet sauce made from beaten eggs, Marsala and sugar.

Preserves

Preserves are perishable foods to which sugar and/or vinegar and/or other ingredients are added to extend their shelf life and provide delicious accompaniments for a variety of different foods. They include chutneys, pickles, relishes, jams, marmalades and jellies.

CHUTNEY

A sweet and sour condiment originating in India, the literal translation of chatni is 'to lick something in small amounts'. More commonly seen in this country in jars, they are often freshly made in India from a wide variety of ingredients, all based on chopped fruit and/or vegetables, sugar and vinegar.

Mango chutney One of the most popular chutneys and it is excellent with curries! It can be sweet or hot and is made from green unripe mangoes.

Tomato chutney A rich and tangy chutney made from tomatoes, gherkins, chillies and spices.

PICKLE

Like chutney, pickles are eaten as a condiment accompanying cold cuts, curries and cheeses. They consist of vegetables and fruit preserved in strongly flavoured vinegar. It is essential to use good quality vinegar with an acidity of at least 5%. White vinegar will show off the colour and texture of pickles, but malt vinegar gives a better flavour.

Single ingredient pickles

These are pickles where there is only one major ingredient.

Caper Capers are the green unopened buds of a shrub native to the Mediterranean. They are only used in their salted or pickled form as a flavouring or condiment.

Olive A fruit of the tree native to the Mediterranean coast. They come in several different varieties and are used only in their pickled form either in recipes or as a snack with drinks.

Pickled cabbage Red or white cabbage shredded and pickled in spiced vinegar.

Pickled eggs Shelled hard-boiled eggs are cooled and then pickled in spiced and seasoned vinegar. Best eaten between one and three months after pickling.

Pickled gherkins These miniature cucumbers are grown especially for pickling and are used as an accompaniment to cold meats or eaten on their own as a cocktail savoury.

Pickled onions Best eaten with cheese, the special pickling onions are first put in brine, then in vinegar.

Pickled walnuts Immature walnuts with the shell still soft are preserved in a solution of vinegar, caramel, black pepper and other spices.

Other pickles

Lime pickle A highly spiced mixture of limes, mustard seeds, fenugreek and other spices. Delicious with curries and poppadoms.

Mango pickle A rather unattractive brown colour, this pickle is a spicy mixture of mangoes, chillies and spices and is eaten with bland foods.

Mixed pickles A mixture of gherkins, cauliflower and onions in a vinegar solution. It is a good accompaniment to cold meat and cheese.

Piccalilli This pickle resembles chutney and contains cauliflower, gherkins and onion blended in a mustard sauce.

Sweet pickle A wide variety of fruit and vegetables can be used to make this pickle which is comparatively sweet in taste, rather like a chutney.

143

RELISH

Relishes are similar to pickles
but generally do not contain
enough vinegar and/or sugar
to preserve the ingredients
for longer than a month.

Cucumber relish A sweet-tasting mixture of cucumbers, mustard seed,
sugar, vinegar, onions, peppers and spices which is a
good accompaniment to cold meat, cheeses and grills.

Gentleman's relish/patum peperium A British commercial preparation
which is brown in colour and based on anchovies and
butter, and is used mainly as a spread on canapes or on
toast as a savoury at the end of a meal.

Horseradish relish Horseradish is a brown root vegetable looking
rather like a parsnip. The grated flesh of the
horseradish is combined with vinegar, cream, salt and
agar-agar to make a relish. It is hot and pungent and is
traditionally served with roast beef. It is also served
with other cold meats, often mixed with cream to
make horseradish sauce, and is popular in Scandinavia
with marinated fish.

Indonesian relish The main ingredients are cabbage, onions, leeks,
carrots and cucumber and it is mainly eaten with
smoked fish.

Japanese pickled relish The Japanese daikon radish, a swollen root, is
sliced thinly, preserved in a solution of soy sauce and
sugar and eaten traditionally with fish.

JAM

Jam is a preserve made by boiling water, fruit and sugar
until the required setting point is reached. A good set is
determined by the amount of pectin and acid in the
fruit, which then reacts with the sugar to give a gel.
The level of pectin and acid varies in different fruits,
therefore some fruits require the addition of extra
pectin and acid, provided by lemon juice, to give a
firmer set. Examples of fruits rich in pectin include
blackcurrants and cherries, while fruits requiring extra
pectin and acid include strawberries, apricots and
raspberries.

MARMALADE

Marmalades are made in the same way as jams but always contain one or more citrus fruits where the rind is suspended in the mixture. As citrus fruit is rich in pectin, the setting point is easily reached. Seville oranges are the most commonly used ingredient for marmalade but delicious alternatives include lemons, limes and grapefruit.

JELLY

Jellies are made by cooking fruit and then straining the juice through a jelly bag or muslin sieve to obtain a clear liquid. This is then heated with sugar to allow the jelly to set. Fruits particularly suited for making jellies include crab apple, quince, redcurrant and cranberry.

Sugars, syrups and honey

WHITE SUGARS

Caster sugar   A very fine crystallised sugar which dissolves quickly in water and is used in cake making and desserts.

Cube sugar/cubed sugar   White or brown sugar crystals that have been compressed into square blocks, and are used to sweeten beverages.

Glucose   Commercial glucose is available as a powder, a syrup and in chips. Used in confectionery and in jam.

Granulated sugar   A white refined sugar with slightly larger granules than caster sugar.

Icing sugar   Refined white sugar that has been pulverized into a fine powder with the addition of cornstarch to prevent the formation of lumps in damp conditions. Used in baking and confectionery, and sifted over desserts and baked goods for a decorative finish.

Jam sugar   Contains added natural apple pectin for making soft fruit jams and jellies.

Loaf sugar   Similar to cube sugar but compressed into a large block.

Preserving sugar   Sugar boiled in a refinery to obtain a large crystal. Used in making preserves and jellies as the larger crystal helps to eliminate scum when boiling.

HANDY HINT

Vanilla sugar

Add a vanilla pod to 1lb of castor sugar, allow one week for the flavour to develop and use in custards, cakes and puddings. Keep in a warm dry place.

Barbados sugar See *muscovado sugar*.

Candy sugar   Large, white refined sugar crystals which are sometimes treated with vegetable dyes to give a variety of colours. It is used to sweeten beverages.

Demerara   Refined white sugar with relatively large crystals treated with light-coloured molasses, with no additional colour added.

Jaggery   Dark and coarse unrefined sugar processed from the sap of palm trees or sugar-cane. It is used in India for making sweets.

Lump sugar   Concentrated dark brown sugar obtainable in blocks and used in Chinese and Indian dishes.

Molasses sugar The colour of this moist and soft sugar is determined by the amount of molasses it contains. It is used in rich dark fruit cakes. The very dark variety is known as black Barbados.

Muscovado sugar Also known as Barbados sugar, this sugar is lighter brown than molasses sugar, and is used in many Indian dishes and fruit cakes. It is available in light or dark varieties according to the molasses colour.

Soft brown sugar Refined white sugar with added cane sugar syrup or molasses. It can be obtained in light and dark varieties, and is usually slightly drier than muscovado or Barbados sugar.

SYRUPS

Black treacle This is a by-product of sugar refining and the darker the syrup the less sugar it contains.

Cane sugar syrup This concentrated sap of the sugar cane is sometimes substituted for molasses.

Cassis syrup   A rich syrup made with sugar and the juice from blackcurrants.

Corn syrup   Produced from maize or sweetcorn. Used in the same way as golden syrup.

HANDY HINT

Measuring syrup

Lightly flour the spoon or scales first as this allows the syrup to slide off without sticking. 1 level tablespoon of syrup weighs approximately 1oz.

Golden syrup Clarified molasses residue.

Maple syrup This distinctive to the taste syrup is the processed sap of the maple tree.

Molasses Slightly bitter in taste, it is often used in the making of very rich fruitcakes where it improves the keeping quality.

HONEY

Honey is a natural product produced by bees from nectar gathered from the flowers of plants. It contains glucose and fructose and is a healthy alternative to cane sugar. The colour and flavour of the honey is dependent on the plants from which the nectar is gathered. The consistency of the honey is determined by whether or not the honey is heat-treated to preserve the clear runny character. Thick honey is honey which has naturally crystallised. Particularly good varieties include clover, lavender, acacia, heather and orange-blossom.

HANDY HINT

Softening hard honey and hard brown sugar

Stand honey that has gone hard in a bowl of hot water to loosen it up, or microwave for 30 secs. Soften hard brown sugar by placing in the microwave for a few seconds.

Oils and vinegars

OILS

Almond oil This oil extracted from almonds has a strong flavour and is delicious used in salad dressings.

Avocado oil This oil is taken from the damaged flesh of avocados and is a good cooking oil.

Coconut oil An excellent frying oil extracted from the white flesh of the coconut.

Corn oil Made from the sweetcorn plant, this oil is used for making margarine and is commonly used for cooking. It is particularly good for shallow or deep-frying, having one of the highest smoking points. The smoking point is the temperature at which smoke is produced, and oils with a high smoking point are best for frying.

Cottonseed oil Oil from the seeds of the cotton plant. It can be used as a salad oil or as a constituent in vegetable cooking oil.

Extra virgin/virgin/olive oil The best of all the oils, the flavour varies from country to country. Spanish olive oil has the strongest flavour, Italian a nutty flavour, Greek a heavy texture and French a fruity taste. The modern mills where the pressure is applied mechanically have replaced the traditional method of crushing the olives. 'Cold pressing' and 'first pressing' are rarely mentioned today as only one pressing is required by the modern method and no heat is required to extract the oil.

The most superior of all the olive oils is virgin oil, this is separated into two grades, extra virgin with a one per cent acidity, and virgin which has a two per cent acidity. Virgin can usually be identified by its greenish colour but may also be golden yellow. The best virgin oils come from green Provençal or Tuscan olives, especially from the town of Lucca. Olive oils or 'pure' olive oils have a blander taste, are paler in colour, and are blended from different olives with a little virgin olive oil added to improve the flavour.

Grapeseed oil This oil is best known for its use in fondue bourguignonne, where its light, aromatic flavour does not taint the meat.

Groundnut oil/peanut oil A popular substitute for olive oil in France when cooking, particularly for frying as it has very little smell or flavour. The Chinese add fresh ginger, garlic or spring onion to this oil before use.

Hazelnut oil Oil extracted from the hazelnut. It is delicious in salad dressings.

Palm oil Oil extracted from the seed of the palm fruit. It is used primarily in the manufacture of margarine, in African and Brazilian cooking and as an ingredient in vegetable oil.

Rapeseed oil This oil is popular in the United States as it is low in saturated fats, with only olive oil having more mono-unsaturated fat. Rapeseed oil is also used in blends with other oils to make margarine.

Safflower oil Low in cholesterol, often confused with sunflower, safflower oil comes from the thistle-like safflower plant. This oil is used in the same way and is very light in flavour.

Sesame oil The thicker and darker this oil is, the more aromatic it is. The dark oil is made from toasted sesame seeds and is used more for flavouring as it burns easily.

Soya bean oil This oil is the main constituent in blended oils, cooking fat and margarine.

Sunflower oil Sunflower oil is light, mild and thin, making it excellent for cooking.

Vegetable oil A blended mixture of coconut, rapeseed, soya bean, palm and cottonseed oils. Excellent for use in cooking because of its high smoking point and little taste.

Walnut oil Strong and with a delicious nutty flavour, this oil, mixed with a lighter one, makes a great dressing for a spinach salad. This oil should be kept in the fridge and not stored for any length of time. It is not a suitable oil to use in cooking.

Balsamic vinegar Made from the must (unfermented concentrated juice) of white Trebbiano grapes from the Modena region of Italy. The must is boiled until thick and then matured in barrels. These barrels are made from oak, chestnut, mulberry, hornbeam, cherry or other woods. Every year for the first five years, as evaporation takes place, the vinegar is moved to a smaller barrel. It may then be left to age for anything from a further five to fifty years .

Cider vinegar Excellent for making pickles and chutneys, especially apple chutney. It is also used as an aid for digestion and to prevent hair loss!

Distilled vinegar Colourless vinegar made by distilling any vinegar, usually malt. It is used mainly for pickling, especially silver onions where the finished colour is important.

Flavoured vinegar Wine vinegar can be flavoured by adding fresh herbs, such as tarragon, basil, mint and thyme. It is kept in a warmish place for a week, after which it is decanted, and a token sprig of the herb is put into the bottle.

Fruit vinegar A wine vinegar flavoured with a soft fruit such as raspberry, strawberry or blackcurrant.

Malt vinegar This vinegar is brewed from malted barley and coloured with caramel to varying degrees of brown. The best of malts has at least five per cent acidity and is excellent for pickling, and great with fish and chips.

Rice vinegar The sweet delicate flavour of this vinegar is popular in South East Asian cooking, especially in Japan.

Sherry vinegar Made from sweet sherry, this vinegar varies in strength. At its best it can rival balsamic vinegar in flavour.

Spirit vinegar Made from molasses or sugar beet alcohol, and may be used for pickling as it is colourless.

Wine vinegar Wine vinegar can be red or white and can vary in strength whilst remaining delicious. You can dilute a very strong one by adding the same coloured wine.

Cuisines around the world

Cuisines around the world

AFRICAN

Ackara A Gambian dish served seven days after the birth of a child, at the naming ceremony. It consists of soaked white beans finely ground, then worked into a stiff paste with water. The mixture is then shaped into balls and deep-fried and served with a tomato, onion, pepper, garlic and chilli sauce.

Aloco Fried plantain with a hot tomato sauce.

Berbere An Ethiopean seasoning of paprika, chilli and other spices.

Cassava A coarse root that is boiled and pounded to make bread and other foods.

Egusi Ground melon seeds, which are then added to stews and soups.

Fufu A stiff pudding made from maize or pounded yam.

Ground rice A stiff rice pudding which accompanies soup.

Jollof rice Traditionally a hot spicy risotto made with tomatoes, onions and sometimes chicken.

Injera A spongy bread.

Kelewele/do-do Fried plantain.

Ogbono Large seed similar to egusi and used in much the same way.

Suya A spicy Nigerian meat kebab.

Tuo/tuwo A stiff rice pudding shaped into balls and served with soup.

Ugali A Tanzanian stew traditionally made with goat and served with maize porridge.

Wot A thick dark sauce made from slowly cooked onions, garlic, butter and spices. It is one of the basic ingredients in most stews.

Waakye Rice and black-eyed beans mixed with meat or chicken in gravy.

Waaste Rice and black-eyed beans cooked together.

CARIBBEAN

Accra A Trinidadian yeasted and fried doughnut made from salt cod.

Ackra fritters Jamaican fritters made from mashed black-eyed beans and chillies.

Acra lamori Fishcakes from St Lucia made from salt cod and deep-fried.

Ackee A red-skinned fruit with yellow flesh, traditionally served in a Jamaican dish of salt cod, onion and peppers.

Breadfruit A cross between a sweet potato and a chestnut, this football-sized fruit has sweet, creamy flesh.

Callalo The spinach-like leaves of various vegetables used as a base in a soup with pork or crabmeat.

Carne mechada A boiled stuffed beef roll from Cuba and the Dominican Republic. It is served sliced with the puréed liquid in which it was cooked.

Cassava A fleshy tuber of a plant which grows as a cylindrical and swollen root.

Conkies/paimi Steamed sweet or savoury cornmeal and coconut wrapped in plantain or banana leaves.

Coo-coo A cake, similar to polenta, made from cornmeal and okra.

Crab backs Crabmeat, fried onions, tomatoes, Worcestershire sauce, vinegar and seasonings stuffed in a crabshell and baked until brown.

Festival A deep-fried slightly sweet dumpling served with fried fish.

Floats Yeasted bread, traditionally from Trinidad, rolled into thin rounds, fried and served hot.

Foo-foo A Barbadian dish of pounded plantain, rolled into balls and served hot.

Escovitch fish Fish fried or grilled and then pickled in a tangy sauce.

Jerk chicken/jerk pork The meat is marinated in chilli and hot spices and slowly roasted or barbecued.

Jug-jug Caribbean stew containing fresh or salted beef, pork and pigeon pea purée.

Pastelillos Meat or cheese deep-fried pastries, served as an appetiser.

Peas/beans Another name for black-eyed beans, black beans, green peas and red kidney beans.

Pelau A version of pilaf, made from chicken and salt beef, almonds, sugar, water, butter, olives, rice, onions, tomatoes, herbs, spices and seasonings.

Pepperpot A meat or vegetable stew containing cassava.

Pigeon pea A legume, used either fresh as a vegetable or dried as a pulse.

Plantain A variety of banana which is cooked in the same way as potato.

Roti Indian bread which is usually filled with meat or vegetable curry.

Soursop A dark green, spiny fruit.

Sweet potato A tuberous root with a sweetish taste.

Yam A large tuber with yellowish or white flesh which has a slightly nutty flavour.

CENTRAL AND EASTERN EUROPEAN

Bigos Hunter's stew made with sauerkraut, various meats and sausage, mushrooms and juniper berries.

Blini Yeast-leavened pancake made from buckwheat flour, traditionally served with butter and sour cream.

Borscht Classic beetroot soup garnished with sour cream, boiled egg or little dumplings.

Caviar The most highly prized is the fish roe from the sturgeon, closely followed in descending order by beluga, oscietra and sevruga, although salmon or keta caviar is underrated.

Chlodnik A chilled, bright pink beetroot soup garnished with sour cream.

Galabki/golubsty These cabbage parcels are either stuffed with meat, rice or kasha.

Golonka Pork knuckle more often cooked in beer.

Kasha/kasza Buckwheat, which when roasted has a delicious, light nutty flavour.

Kaszanka Blood sausage made with buckwheat.

Knedliky Bread dumplings.

Kolduny Small meat-filled dumplings often served in borscht.

Kotlet schabowy Breaded pork chops.

Coulebiac/koulebiak Layered salmon pie with eggs, rice and mushrooms.

Latke Fried grated potato pancakes.

Makowiec Poppyseed cake.

Mizeria Very thinly sliced cucumber dressed with sour cream.

Nalesniki Cream cheese pancakes.

Paczki Doughnuts traditionally filled with plum jam.

Pelmeni Siberian-style ravioli dumplings.

Pierogi Ravioli-style dumplings, traditionally filled with sauerkraut and mushroom, curd cheese or fruit.

Pirogi Large filled pies made with a yeasty dough.

Pirozhki Small version of pirogi.

Sashlik Caucasian spit-roasted meat.

Shchi Soup made from sauerkraut.

Stroganoff Strips of beef in a rich sour cream and mushroom sauce.

Surowka Raw shredded vegetable salad.

Ushka Small ear-shaped dumplings traditionally served in soup.

Vareniki Ukranian-style ravioli dumplings filled with sauerkraut.

Zakuski/zakaski A combination of many dishes covering a table, including pickles, marinated vegetables and fish, herrings, smoked eel, aspic, mushrooms, radishes and caviar.

Zrazy Beef rolls stuffed with bacon, pickled cucumber and mustard.

Zurek Sour rye soup.

CHINESE

Bird's nest soup Edible nests of swifts from Southern Asian, made from seaweed and saliva, are used to make this soup together with chicken stock, chicken, ham, egg whites, seasoning and cornflour. Not for the faint-hearted!

Chinese egg roll See *spring roll*.

Chop suey A westernised version of a Chinese dish made from shredded meat or chicken, mushrooms, bamboo shoots, onions and bean sprouts. Served with rice and soy sauce.

Chow mein Similar to chop suey but served with noodles and is usually fried.

Dim sum The traditional food eaten for breakfast in Southern China. The literal translation of 'dim sum' is 'little pieces so dear to the heart', which refers to the vast selection of dumplings and other delicacies which Chinese people like to eat, washed down with green tea.

Char siu bao Fluffy steamed bun stuffed with barbecued pork in a sweet-savoury sauce.

Char siu puff pastry/roast pork puff Triangular puff pastry parcel filled with barbequed pork, sprinkled with sesame seeds and cooked in the oven.

Cheung fun Sheets of steamed rice pasta wrapped around king sized prawns, roast pork and splashed with soy-based sweet sauce.

Chiu chow fun gwor Soft steamed dumpling with a wheat starch wrapper, stuffed with pork, vegetables and peanuts.

Har gau A translucent wheat-starch dumpling filled with minced prawns.

Nor mai gai Glutinous rice, pork and mushrooms wrapped in a lotus leaf and steamed.

Paper-wrapped prawns Deep-fried tissue-thin rice paper filled with prawn meat and dusted with sesame seeds.

Scallop dumpling A wheat starch dumpling filled with a combination of scallop and other seafood.

Shark's fin dumpling A small dumpling made from wheat starch, pinched into a frilly cockscomb and filled with minced prawn and pork and, depending on how expensive they are, maybe some shark's fin!

Siu loon bao A speciality from Shanghai, this wheaten wrapper is pinched into a swirl and filled with minced pork.

Siu mai A cup-shaped wheaten dumpling with an open top filled with minced pork and topped with either orange crab roe or grated carrot.

Turnip paste Made from glutinous rice and white radishes studded with fragments of wind-dried pork, sausage and shrimps. It is cut into a slab and sautéed until it is golden in colour.

Yam/taro croquette A deep-fried dumpling in the shape of an egg made with minced pork and mashed taro.

Eggs foo yung Chinese omelettes which have been deep-fried or shallow-fried and are flavoured with spring onions, soy sauce, garlic and sherry. Shredded meat and cooked vegetables are added.

Fried rice Served as an accompaniment to other dishes, spring onions and egg are added to cooked rice and stir-fried in oil.

Hot and sour soup A soup containing shredded pork, vegetables, Chinese dried mushrooms, eggs, soy sauce, vinegar, cornflour and seasonings.

Peking duck A specially prepared duck is roasted until the skin is crispy and the meat is easily removed from the bones. Traditionally served with pancakes brushed with hoisin sauce and rolled up with the duck and strips of spring onion and cucumber. Total heaven!

Prawn crackers These crackers are opaque flat discs which puff up as they are deep-fried and turn an off-white colour. They can be bought already cooked and are served as an accompaniment to Chinese dishes.

Rice wine Made from fermented rice, this Chinese drink is similar in taste to sherry.

Sweet and sour A sauce containing soy sauce, vinegar, sugar, sherry and cornflour is served as an accompaniment to fried pork, poultry or shellfish.

Tahu Chinese equivalent of tofu or bean curd.

Wontons Egg pasta, similar to ravioli, is filled with various fillings of minced fish, meat, vegetables and seasonings and deep-fried. Served as an appetiser or in soup.

FRENCH

Aioli sauce A sauce made of garlic flavoured mayonnaise.

Assiette de charcuterie A plate of assorted cold meats.

Baiser The literal translation means 'kiss', and it is two meringue halves sandwiched together with whipped cream.

Bisque A puréed shellfish soup thickened with cream and egg yolks.

Bitok The French term for a Russian-style meat loaf served with sour cream.

Bombes This is traditionally two different flavoured ice creams set in a conical mould. One is used to line the mould while the other, normally containing glace fruits, nuts and liqueurs, fills the centre.

Bouillabaisse A classic rich fish soup from the Mediterranean.

Bouquet garni The name used for a small bunch of herbs tied together which is used to flavour stews, soups, etc. Usually bay, thyme and parsley are used, although other herbs such as marjoram or tarragon may be added.

Bourride A fish stew served with aioli toast.

Brandade de morue A purée of cooked dried salt cod mixed with milk, olive oil, garlic and lemon juice, delicious served hot with fried bread.

Cassoulet This dish originated in the Languedoc region, and contains haricot beans which are soaked overnight, fresh and smoked pork, smoked sausages, onions and carrots, which are cooked very slowly in the traditional clay pot.

Charlotte A traditional hot fruit pudding.

Clafouti Black cherries baked in a thick, creamy batter in the oven until golden, sprinkled with sugar and eaten with cream whilst still warm.

Coeur à la crème A dessert made from curd which has been drained in a special perforated heart-shaped mould. The soft cheese can also be made using a muslin-lined sieve.

Coulibiac The French name for the Russian fish pie filled with salmon, rice, hard-boiled eggs and cream.

Crêpinette A small flat sausage or a croquette which has been wrapped in bacon and then grilled.

Croque madame See *croque monsieur*.

Croque monsieur A hot cheese and ham sandwich which has been fried in clarified butter. If served topped with a poached egg it is known as a *croque madame*.

Croquembouche An elaborate wedding cake made from cream-filled choux pastry buns coated with caramel and piled up into a pyramid.

Croquette Minced meat, poultry, fish or vegetable is bound together with mashed potatoes and beaten egg, coated in breadcrumbs and fried. The shape of the croquette varies from flat and round to cork shaped to ovals or balls.

Crudités Raw vegetables used for dipping into sauces. Crunchy vegetables such as carrots, celery, cauliflower and green peppers are commonly used.

Daube A rich casserole made from marinated meat, root vegetables, herbs and wine, which has been made in a special lidded earthenware pot known as a daubière.

Dodine Boned poultry or duck stuffed with paté and simmered in wine.

Garbure A thick vegetable soup containing beans and preserved meat, which is ladled over slices of bread. The remaining few spoonfuls of each serving are sometimes mixed with the remaining mouthful of wine left in each person's glass.

Madeleines Vanilla-flavoured sponge cakes baked in special madeleine moulds.

Marquise A frozen desert made from an alcoholic sorbet and whipped cream.

Navarin A lamb stew cooked with root vegetables, green beans and tomatoes.

Petit marmite A meat and vegetable soup served in a lidded earthenware pot.

Pipérade Scrambled eggs made with chopped tomato, ham and peppers.

Pissaladière A Provençal version of pizza.

Pistou A Provençal version of pesto.

Pot au feu Beef boiled in a vegetable soup. It is generally used for two courses, the meat and vegetables are served together and the remaining rich broth is used as soup.

Potée A soup containing cabbage, potatoes, beans, lentils, salt pork and sausages.

Quenelles A purée of fish, meat, chicken or game containing egg whites and whipped cream is lightly poached in stock by the spoonful and served coated with a rich sauce.

Ratatouille A Provençal vegetable stew containing onions, peppers, tomatoes, aubergines, courgettes and garlic.

Rillettes A rich meat paté which is made by simmering pork in its own fat until very tender, pounding until fairly smooth and packing into small earthenware pots.

Savarin A yeasted cake baked in a ring-shaped mould and steeped in rum-flavoured syrup. The centre is filled with whipped cream and fruits.

Vacherin A cake layered up with rings of meringue and whipped cream.

Bismark herrings Fresh boned herrings, marinated overnight in vinegar, herbs and spices.

Black Forest ham A superior air-dried ham from Southern Germany with a strong smoky flavour, usually served with a potato salad.

Blutwurst A sausage similar to black pudding and made from pork, pig's blood, pieces of fat and seasonings. It is thickened with cereal and sometimes flavoured with onion, cut into thick slices and fried, and traditionally served with creamed potatoes and stewed apple.

Bockwurst A scalded sausage, which is similar to the frankfurter but slightly more plump and spicy.

Bratwurst A sausage made from veal or pork, which is fried or grilled.

Dresdener Christollen A yeasted and fruited Christmas cake, similar to stollen.

Eisbein Pickled boiled pig's knuckles which are served hot with sauerkraut and potatoes.

Extrawurst A scalded fine-textured sausage made from well-spiced beef and pork which is pale pink in colour. It may be sliced and eaten cold in a salad or used in stews.

Frankfurter A smooth-textured scalded sausage made from the best pork which is cold-smoked to give the sausage a golden colour.

Himmel und Erde A speciality dish consisting of creamed potato served with apple purée and fried onions then topped with fried liver. The literal translation means 'heaven and earth'!

Kartoffelpuffer Large potato cake served hot with cold apple purée.

Kassler Loin of pork which has been lightly smoked with juniper berries. It can be roasted, cut into slices and fried or thinly carved and used as an appetiser. Hot Kassler is served with creamed potatoes or noodles and pease pudding.

Klosse/knodel Dumplings made from potato, flour, breadcrumbs or semolina, mixed with fat and milk. The dumplings are boiled and served with sweet or savoury dishes.

Kopenhagener The German name for Danish pastries.

Labskaus A hash made from mashed potato, onion, chopped corned beef and seasoning. Each portion is topped with a fried egg and accompanied by pickled beetroot and gherkin.

Leberkasse A pre-cooked meat loaf from Bavaria, similar to luncheon meat in appearance, containing minced liver and sausage meat. It is cut into thick slices which are grilled or fried.

Leberknodelsuppe A classic Bavarian clear soup containing small dumplings made from breadcrumbs, liver and herbs, garnished with finely chopped parsley or chives.

Leberwurst Liver sausage.

Lebkuchen Spicy ginger biscuits, often covered with white icing or chocolate, which are traditionally eaten around Christmas from Advent to Twelfth Night.

Matjes Small herrings which have been lightly cured, served with raw onion and boiled potatoes.

Pfannkuchen Pancakes which tend to be slightly thicker than the French and English versions.

Pretzel Dry, slightly salty savoury biscuit made into various shapes, most commonly figures of eight.

Quark A low fat, soft cow's milk cheese, similar to a smooth cottage cheese. It has a fresh mild taste, which makes it suitable for either sweet or savoury dishes.

Sauerbraten A dish made from beef which has been marinated for up to three days in spiced vinegar, then cooked with vegetables and ginger cake or biscuits to give it a sweet-sour taste.

Sauerkraut Finely-shredded pickled white cabbage which may be eaten hot or cold.

Spatzel Egg noodles from Southern Germany and the Alsace region of France.

Stollen A yeasted Christmas cake filled with fruit, nuts and marzipan which is folded like an omelette, baked and then thickly coated with melted butter and sifted icing sugar.

Wurst Sausage.

GREAT BRITAIN

Angels on horseback Smoked or raw oysters wrapped in streaky bacon and grilled.

Arbroath smokies Scottish smoked haddock.

Bannock Shortbread containing chopped mixed peel and almonds, a speciality of Scotland.

Bara brith A yeasted Welsh loaf containing fruit.

Bath chap The lower part of the pig's cheek including the jaw bone, half the tongue and snout which is pickled, boiled and boned and coated in breadcrumbs.

Blaa Sausage rolls from Waterford in Ireland.

Black pudding A cooked sausage made traditionally from pig's blood and thickened with cereal.

Blind Scouse A hot pot made from vegetables and potatoes, originally from Lancashire.

Bloxty A filled pancake.

Brawn Pieces of meat from the pig's head set in a savoury jelly.

Brose A thin porridge eaten in Scotland with butter, milk or cream.

Bubble and squeak Leftover mashed potato and chopped cabbage pan-fried in lard or dripping to form a shallow crisp cake.

Buck rarebit Welsh rarebit topped with a poached egg.

Carrigeen Seaweed dish from Ireland.

Cawl Substantial meat and vegetable broth from Wales.

Champ Northern Irish mashed potato made with spring onions.

Civet A dark brown stew made from rabbit or hare.

Clootie dumpling A Scottish pudding made from spices, dried fruit, sugar, suet, flour, breadcrumbs and milk.

Cock-a-leekie soup A Scottish chicken and leek soup containing rice.

Colcannon Irish dish made from mashed potato, cabbage and onion fried in butter.

Cornish fairings Crisp butter biscuits made with spices and sweetened with brown sugar and syrup.

Cornish pasty A pastry turnover filled with potato, vegetables and beef.

Cottage pie Cooked minced beef and gravy topped with a thick layer of mashed potato and cooked until golden in the oven.

Cullen skink Flaked Finnan haddock mixed with mashed potato, butter and boiled onions and garnished with chopped parsley.

Dropped scone A thick batter made with a raising agent is dropped onto a heated griddle and cooked until golden on both sides. It is served warm with butter and jam.

Eccles cake Originally from Eccles in Lancashire, it is made from puff pastry filled with currants, mixed chopped peel, butter, brown sugar and spices and brushed with milk and caster sugar before baking.

Fadge Triangular Irish potato cakes made from potato, salt, flour and butter, fried until golden on both sides and sandwiched together with butter.

Faggots Made from salt pork, minced liver, breadcrumbs, finely diced onion and spices and bound together with egg into balls which are wrapped in pig's caul.

Flapjacks Biscuits made from oats, sugar, butter, and syrup.

Flummery Originally a Welsh dessert made from fermented and soured oatmeal mixed with water. The term is more commonly used now for a creamy blancmange.

Forfar bridies Scottish pastry turnovers filled with beef, suet and onions.

Haggis A Scottish delicacy made from sheep's heart, liver and lungs!

Irish stew A stew of mutton, potatoes and onions.

Laver bread Seaweed and oatmeal bread.

Oxford John Lamb steaks cut from the leg, fried with onion, thyme and parsley and served with a gravy.

Pease pudding Split peas that have been mashed with butter, egg yolks and seasoning.

Petticoat tails Scottish shortbread with skirt-shaped edges.

Poor man's goose Faggots.

Scotch broth A thick soup made from lamb, root vegetables and barley.

Scotch woodcock Buttered toast spread with anchovy paste or Gentleman's relish, topped with scrambled egg.

Simnel cake A fruit cake baked with a layer of marzipan in the middle and, when cold, decorated with marzipan, including twelve marzipan balls,

representing the twelve Apostles of Christ.

Spotted dick A pudding made from suet, flour, raising agent, breadcrumbs, dried fruit, sugar, eggs and milk. It is steamed and served traditionally with custard.

Squab pie A pie made with lamb, onions and apple.

Stovies Tasty mash of onion and fried potato heated up with minced beef.

Toad-in-the-hole Sausages cooked in a savoury batter.

Welsh rarebit A cheese mixture grilled on freshly toasted bread.

Yellowman Hard chewy toffee made in County Antrim.

Yorkshire pudding The traditional accompaniment to roast beef, made from a savoury batter.

GREEK CYPRIOT

Afelia Pork stewed in wine and coriander.

Avgolemono Either a sauce made with lemon and eggs or a soup made with lemon, chicken, rice and egg.

Dolmades Vine leaves stuffed with rice, minced meat and spices.

Fasolia A vegetarian bean casserole with tomatoes, oregano and garlic.

Garides King prawns.

Gigantes White haricot beans in tomato sauce.

Halloumi A cheese, usually served grilled.

Horiatiki A Greek salad containing tomato, cucumber, onion, feta cheese, olive oil and sometimes green pepper.

Houmous A dip made from puréed chickpeas, sesame seed paste (tahini), lemon juice and garlic.

Kalamari/calamari Lightly battered and deep-fried squid.

Kataifi Shredded wheat rolls lightly soaked in syrup.

Kefalotyri Hard very salty cheese.

Keftedes Herby meatballs.

Kleftiko Slow roasted shoulder of lamb, flavoured with oregano and other herbs.

Loukanika A spicy sausage marinated in wine and coriander.

Lountza Smoked loin of pork.

Lukumi Turkish Delight.

Marides Little fish similar to whitebait.

Melitzanosalata A salad of mashed aubergine, garlic, olive oil and vinegar.

Meze A selection of hors d'oeuvres and main dishes that can be either hot or cold.

Moussaka A baked dish of layered minced lamb, fried aubergine, vegetables and herbs topped with a béchamel sauce.

Pourgouri Cracked wheat.

Saganaki Either grilled halloumi or kefalotyri cheese, or can apply to anything in a cheese sauce.

Sheftalia Minced and seasoned lamb shaped onto a skewer and char-grilled.

Skordalia Garlic-based dip.

Soutsoukakia Baked meat rissoles topped with a tomato-based sauce.

Souvlaki Traditionally, lamb grilled on a skewer. Outside Greece this dish is commonly known as a shish kebab.

Spanakopitta Small spinach and ricotta pies, more often cooked in filo pastry in the UK.

Stiflado A rich beef or vegetable stew cooked with wine.

Taboulleh A salad made from cracked wheat, chopped parsley, cucumber, tomato and lemon juice.

Taramasalata Nowadays this dish of fish roe paté is made from cod roe, garlic or onion, breadcrumbs, olive oil and lemon juice.

Tavas Meat, onion and herbs cooked in an earthenware dish.

Tzatziki A dip made from yoghurt, lemon juice, grated cucumber, mint and garlic.

Tsakistes Split green olives marinated with lemon, garlic, coriander seeds and other spices.

Tyropitta A feta pie.

INDIAN AND SRI LANKAN

Aloo Potato.

Aloo tikki Flat potato cake with lentil stuffing.

Aluva Rice flour, treacle and cashew nut fudge.

Ambul Thiyal Pickle made from tuna, 'sour fish curry'.

Avial A mixed vegetable curry cooked with coconut and yoghurt, originally from Kerala.

Ayre A white fish from Bengal.

Baigan/brinjal Aubergine.

Balti A West Midlands term for Karahi cooking.

Barfi A dry sweetmeat.

Bateira Quail.

Besan Chick-pea flour.

Bhaji/bhajee Spicy vegetable fritters made from chick-pea flour served as a snack in Northern India.

Bhel poori Originally sold as small snacks from street stalls in Bombay, more often found on a menu as a starter. They generally contain tiny, crisp deep-fried pooris, with puffed rice, deep-fried gram flour vermicelli and topped off with chopped onion and potato mixed with chilli, mint and tamarind.

Bhindi Okra/ladies' fingers.

Bhuna gosht A dry spicy lamb dish.

Biryani A rich risotto made from rice, meat, spices and vegetables.

Bombay duck Raw fish which is cured, dried and salted.

Chaat Southern Indian term for snack.

Channa Chick-peas.

Chapatti A flat whole wheat pancake.

Chutney A sweet and sour thick sauce made from a wide variety of ingredients, all based on chopped fruit and/or vegetables, sugar and vinegar, served with curry.

Dahi Yoghurt.

Dhal A thick lentil curry. In Southern India it is served thinner.

Dhansak A Parsee casserole of meat and lentils.

Dhaniya Coriander.

Dopiaza A term for cooking with onions.

Dosa Very thin, lightly fried rice and lentil flour pancake originally from Southern India. A masala dosa is traditionally served with a hot curry sauce, a bright green coconut chutney and stuffed with a spicy mix of potato and vegetables. Absolute heaven!

Dum A technique where food is simmered slowly in a clay pot sealed with a dough, allowing the spices to permeate.

Egg hopper A small Sri Lankan bowl-shaped pancake with a fried egg.

Falooda A rose syrup flavoured milk drink, often served with vermicelli and ice cream.

Gajjar halwa A sweetmeat made from grated carrot and flavoured with cardamom.

Garam masala A blend of ground hot spices.

Ghee Clarified butter used for frying.

Gobi Cauliflower.

Gosht Lamb.

Gram flour Chick-pea flour.

Gulab jamun Warm sweetmeats served in sugar syrup and brown in colour.

Gurda Kidneys.

Haandi Earthenware cooking pot.

Halwa A sweet similar to fudge.

Harak mas A Sri Lankan beef curry, containing onions, garlic, ginger, vinegar, spices and coconut.

Hopper A Sri Lankan speciality, the hopper is a bowl-shaped pancake made with rice flour and coconut milk and deep-fried until crisp. It is then eaten as an accompaniment to curries or as an appetiser, particularly for breakfast.

Idli Eaten in Southern India for breakfast, these steamed sponges of rice and lentil flour are eaten with sambar and coconut chutney. Definitely to die for!

Jaggery Sri Lankan palm sugar.

Jalebis Spirals of deep-fried sweet batter.

Jalfrezi Marinated in yoghurt and cooked in green chillies, usually chicken.

Jhingri Prawns.

Kachori Spiced mung dhal with coriander and peas wrapped in a crispy pastry, traditionally found in Southern India.

Kalan A Southern Indian thin curry made from butter milk, coconut and mangoes.

Kaleji Liver.

Kalu dodol Coconut milk, jaggery and cashew nuts.

Karahi A wok-like cooking pan similar in appearance to a balti pan.

Kavun Spiced flour and treacle batter cake fried in coconut oil

Khadi A buttermilk gravy made with coconut and cloves.

Kheema Minced lamb.

Kheer North Indian milk rice pudding.

Kiri bath A Sri Lankan thick rice and creamed coconut mixture which is set and cut out into diamonds and served with jaggery or dark brown sugar at festivals.

Kofta Meatballs or vegetable dumplings.

Kool Combi boiled, fried and dried in the sun.

Korma Braised in yoghurt or cream.

Kulfi Milk is thickened by boiling and made into ice cream with pistachio nuts, saffron and sugar.

Lampari/lamprai This Sri Lankan speciality is rice boiled in meat stock, with vegetables, meat and curry spices slowly baked in a banana leaf.

Lassi A yoghurt drink, served either with salt or sugar.

Machli Fish.

Magaz Brain.

Makhani Cooked in butter and sometimes with tomatoes.

Masala With spices.

Massalam Marinated chicken cooked in a casserole.

Mattar/mutter Peas.

Methi Fenugreek.

Moghul Traditional North Indian Muslim dish.

Murgh Chicken.

Nan Tear-drop shaped flat bread cooked in a tandoor oven.

Nihari Lamb shank slowly cooked over a long period.

Pakora The Southern Indian version of the bhaji.

Palak Spinach.

Pan Traditionally eaten sweet or salty as a digestif. A betel leaf is folded into a triangle and stuffed with fennel seeds, betel nuts and coconut.

Paneer Indian curd cheese.

Paat gobi Cabbage.

Patra Similar to a savoury Swiss roll made from a leaf vegetable known as arvi and gram flour from the Southern states.

Paratha A large griddle-fried bread often stuffed with vegetables or minced lamb.

Pasanda Cooked in a similar way to a korma but with thin strips of lamb.

Payasam A reduced milk pudding made with saffron and cardamoms.

Phal Refers to a very hot dish.

Phuul gobi Cauliflower.

Pilau Rice is first cooked in ghee and then water or chicken stock is added together with saffron or, more usually, turmeric.

Pittu A mixture of flour and grated coconut is steamed in a bamboo mould in the shape of a cylinder.

Pol sambul Red, hot-tasting side dish made from grated coconut, chilli and other spices.

Poori A deep-fried circle of whole wheat bread which puffs up during cooking.

Popadom Large thin wafers eaten with relishes as a starter.

Punjabi Traditionally a thick stew cooked in a tandoor originating from the Punjabi region.

Raita Yoghurt and cucumber.

Rasam A traditional Southern Indian hot and sour consommé made from lentils.

Ras malai Sour milk and flour patties served in sweet and thickened milk.

Rasgullas Sour milk and flour balls in syrup and served cold.

Roghan gosht Lamb cooked in a rich spicy sauce.

Roti A small parcel of anything from chilli and onion to bacon and egg wrapped in an elasticated dough pancake.

Saag/sag Spinach.

Sambar A hot lentil sauce made with chillies, tamarind and diced vegetables.

Samosa A triangular shaped parcel of pastry filled with vegetables and/or meat.

Saunf Aniseed and other spices served at the end of a meal.

Seekh kebab Skewered and grilled meat.

Shirkhand A very sweet paste made from concentrated yoghurt and saffron.

String hoppers A Sri Lankan speciality, they are nests of noodles which are steamed and used as a curry dip, most commonly at breakfast.

Tak-a-tak Meat which is chopped while cooking on a griddle.

Talapia A freshwater fish.

Tamarind The seeds of this tree may be made into a sour-tasting paste which is used in many curries.

Tandoor A North Indian clay oven in which food is cooked without oil.

Tandoori A term applied for a dish cooked in a tandoor oven, often marinated in yoghurt first.

Tarka A traditional Bengali technique where spices and flavourings are cooked separately and added to the dish in the final stages.

Thali The literal translation is plate, which consists of rice, bread, dhal, yoghurt and a variety of vegetable curries.

Thambili A Sri Lankan speciality, milk from the king coconut drunk directly from the shell.

Tikka Meat cut into cubes, marinated in yoghurt with spices and baked in a tandoor.

Uthappam A spicy, crisp pancake made with lentil and rice flour topped with tomato and chillies.

Vadai Fritters of ground lentils, similar in look to a doughnut and served with yoghurt and a tamarind and date sauce, a delicacy of the South.

Varak Indian silver leaf which is used for decorative purposes.

Vindaloo Authentic vindaloos should be cooked with garlic and vinegar for a slightly sour taste, originally from Goa.

Watlalappam Sri Lankan egg pudding tasting of caramel.

ITALIAN

All'Amatriciana Dishes which contain a tomato-flavoured sauce with chopped onions and salt pork or bacon, served with pasta, meat or poultry dishes.

Amaretti Small macaroon biscuits which contain almonds and are usually served with coffee at the end of a meal.

Antipasti The term Italians use for appetisers.

Arance caramellate A dessert of oranges coated with a caramel syrup and decorated with strips of orange peel.

Bollito misto A speciality where various meats, most commonly beef, veal and chicken, are boiled together with vegetables, herbs and spices. The liquid is served separately as soup with pastini and the meats as a main course with potatoes and horseradish.

Brodo di manzo A clear beef broth usually containing pastini.

Calzone A large baked turnover made from yeasted pizza dough, usually containing cheese and ham.

Cappuccino Coffee made by the espresso method with the addition of hot foaming milk.

Cassata A minimum of three differently flavoured and coloured ice-creams which are frozen together in layers.

Cassata alla Siciliana A multi-layered chocolate cake, soaked in liqueur, filled with ricotta cheese and decorated with glacé fruits and nuts.

Espresso A strong bitter coffee which is made from dark-roasted ground beans by using super-heated steam, produced under pressure.

Fonduta Italian version of the Swiss fondue.

Frittata Italian-style vegetable omelette which is fried on both sides and served flat.

Fritto misto di mare Small pieces of assorted fish, seafood and vegetables which have been fried or deep-fried.

Gnocchi Dumplings made from either semolina, potato or choux paste, sometimes covered in a tomato sauce, topped with grated cheese and browned in the oven.

Granita A type of water ice made from coffee or fruit juice and served half frozen.

Grissini Thin crisp bread sticks.

Lasagne pasticciate The name given to a dish made from lasagne pasta.

Minestrone Classic soup made from meat, vegetables, pasta and dried beans topped with a sprinkling of grated Parmesan cheese.

Osso Bucco A speciality from Lombardy which consists of shin of veal, cut into slices, cooked in a tomato and wine sauce with vegetables and stock. Each portion is sprinkled with a mixture of parsley, garlic and grated lemon peel and traditionally served with risotto alla Milanese.

Pannetone A yeasted cake from Milan containing nuts, sultanas and spices.

Peperonata A vegetable stew, similar to ratatouille, made from red peppers, tomatoes, onion, garlic and herbs.

Piccata Thin slices of veal escalope, fried and served with lemon.

Pizza A flat, open tart made from a yeasted bread dough topped with a variety of savouries.

Polenta A coarse version of semolina, made with yellow maize, which is cooked with water until thick. It is served with meat dishes or simply eaten on its own topped with butter and grated Parmesan.

Pollo alla cacciatora A chicken stew consisting of tomatoes, Marsala, stock and mushrooms.

Pollo alla marengo A chicken stew containing tomatoes, stock, white wine, mushrooms, parsley and black olives.

Risi e bisi An appetiser made from cooked rice and peas and served with grated Parmesan.

Risotto A savoury rice dish.

Saltimbocca Rolls of very thin slices of veal with ham and sage leaves fried in butter.

Scaloppine Thin slices of veal or pork fillet, which are coated in either breadcrumbs or flour and fried in butter, traditionally served with a tomato sauce.

Stracciatella A classic soup from Rome where a mixture of beaten eggs, semolina and grated parmesan is whisked into the boiling beef or chicken broth.

Stufato Beef braised with red wine, onions, celery, tomatoes, garlic and ham.

Vitello tonnato Cold roast veal coated in a tuna, mayonnaise and lemon sauce and served with lemon.

Zabaglione A very light foamy dessert made from Marsala, egg yolks and sugar which is served warm.

JAPANESE

Amaebi Sweet shrimps.

Bento A meal served in a compartmentalised box.

Calpis/calpico A milk-based soft sweet drink, similar in taste to barley water and diluted to taste.

Cha-soba Japanese buckwheat noodles to which powdered green tea has been added.

Chawan mushi Savoury egg custard served in a tea tumbler known as a chawan.

Daikon A long white radish, also known as mooli, often grated or cut into fine strips.

Dango Japanese dumpling.

Dashi A basic stock for soups and sauces made from bonito (a type of tuna) flakes and kelp.

Dobin mushi Prawns, fish, chicken, shiitake and ginko nuts in a lightly flavoured dashi-based soup served in a dobin, a clay teapot.

Donburi A bowl of rice served with a topping of beef, chicken or egg.

Edamame Fresh soybeans boiled in their pods and sprinkled with salt.

Gari Traditionally served with sushi, this pinkish, thinly-sliced pickled ginger is used to cleanse the palate between courses.

Gohan Rice.

Gohanmono Japanese term for all rice dishes.

Gyoza Steamed soft rice pastry cases stuffed with minced pork and herbs and then deep-fried.

Hashi Chopsticks.

Hiyashi Chuks Chinese-style ramen served cold in tsuyu with a mixed topping that usually includes shredded ham, chicken, cucumber, egg and beansprouts.

Ikura Salmon roe.

Katsu Breaded and deep-fried meat.

Kinoko Mushroom.

Maki A literal translation means roll. This style of sushi is where the rice and filling are rolled inside a nori wrapper.

Manju A Japanese cake eaten at tea-time with green tea.

Menrui A Japanese name for all types of noodles.

Mirin A sweetened rice wine used in many Japanese sauces and dressings.

Miso A thick paste of fermented soybeans used in miso soup.

Mushimono Japanese word for steaming.

Nabemono A class of dishes cooked at the table in earthenware pots or metal pans.

Natto Fermented soybeans of stringy consistency.

Nimono Vegetables boiled in a stock and served dry.

Nori Sheets of dried seaweed.

Okashi Japanese term for sweets and desserts.

Ponzu A mixture of citrus juices and soya sauce used as a dip.

Ramen Chinese-style egg noodles

Robatayaki A grilled food usually cooked in front of the customer.

Sake A rice wine usually served warm, between 15% and 16% alcohol.

Sashimi Raw fish.

Shiso A nettle-like leaf of the mint family often served with sashimi.

Shochu A colourless alcoholic drink made from a variety of wheat, rice and potatoes, similar to vodka.

Shoyu Japanese soy sauce.

Soba Buckwheat noodles.

Somen Thin, white wheat flour noodles.

Sukiyaki Pieces of thinly cut beef and vegetables that are boiled at the table and dipped in egg when taken out. The hot food partially cooks the egg.

Sunomono A Japanese salad dressed

with vinegar and served in small portions as an appetiser or at the end of a formal meal.

Sushi A combination of raw fish, shellfish or vegetables with rice. Sugar-sweetened vinegar is often added to the rice, which is then cooled before use. Nigir is lozenge-shaped, futomaki is thick rolled, temaki is hand rolled, gunkan makinigiri is wrapped in nori, and chirashi is scattered on top of a bowl of rice.

Teishoku A set meal.

Tempura Fish, shellfish or vegetables dipped in a light batter and deep-fried.

Teppanyaki Means 'grilled on an iron plate'. Nowadays, a chef stands at a hot plate surrounded by eight or so diners who watch the beef, fish and vegetables being artfully sliced and cooked in a theatrical way in front of them.

Teriyaki A sauce made from a thick reduction of shoyu, sake, sugar and spices. It is also the name for the method in which the meat is marinated in shoyu and wine then grilled and served with this sauce.

Tofu Soy bean curd.

Udon Thick, white wheat flour noodles.

Wafu Japanese-style.

Wakame Seaweed.

Wasabi/mountain hollyhock A hot mustard, green in colour, similar to horseradish.

Yakitori Grilled chicken parts.

Yakimono Anything grilled.

Zensaui Hors d'oeuvres.

JEWISH

Bagels Ring-shaped rolls of sweet heavy bread, the dough for which is first boiled or steamed then glazed and baked.

Blintzes Pancakes, traditionally filled with cream cheese and folded into a parcel, but can also be filled with anything sweet or savoury.

Borscht Classic beetroot soup, served either hot or cold and topped with a dollop of sour cream.

Challah Sabbath bread, made from yeasted dough with the addition of eggs, shaped like a plait and sprinkled with poppy seeds.

Charoset A condiment of chopped apples, walnuts, wine and cinnamon served during Passover.

Cholent This rich meat and bean stew is traditionally cooked overnight and served on the Sabbath.

Cholla A very rich bread made from yeasted dough.

Chopped egg and onion An appetiser made from chopped hard-boiled eggs, chopped onion, melted chicken fat and seasonings.

Chopped liver Chicken or calf's liver fried with onions, coarsely chopped and mixed with hard-boiled eggs whites to form a thick pate. This is then moistened with chicken fat and topped with hard-boiled egg before serving.

Chrain A strong sauce made from grated horseradish and beetroot and eaten as a relish with fish.

Farfel Pellet-shaped pasta.

Falafel Spicy balls of ground chick-pea deep-fried and usually served with houmous and pitta bread.

Gefilte fish A fish stuffing originally made from pike or carp; nowadays haddock or cod is mixed with onion, celery, carrots, egg and meal and rolled into balls which are boiled or fried and traditionally served cold.

Gildeneh yoich Traditional chicken soup.

Hamantaschen Small, sweet triangular pastries filled with black poppy seeds, walnuts, syrup, raisins, butter and milk. These are traditionally eaten during the festival of Purim or the Feast of Lots in February or March.

Heimishe Home-cooked Jewish food found in Eastern Europe.

Holishkes Meat and rice stuffed vine or cabbage leaves that are poached in a sweet and sour tomato sauce.

Kishka A vegetable haggis made of flour, barley, onions, carrot and chicken fat which is stuffed into intestines, boiled and baked.

Kneidlach Matzo meal dumplings served in chicken soup.

Kosher Food prepared according to Orthodox Jewish dietary laws.

Kreplach Parcels of noodle dough filled with meat and served in soup. They can also be made with sweet fillings, browned in butter and served with sour cream.

Kugel A savoury made from potatoes, onions and chicken fat and eaten as an accompaniment to meat dishes.

Latkes Grated potatoes, eggs and flour shaped into small pancakes and fried until golden, eaten as a side dish with meat or fish.

Lokshen Egg noodles used in puddings or soups.

Lox Smoked salmon.

Matzos Large, square unleavened water biscuits made from matzo meal.

Petcha A traditional appetiser of calf's foot jelly studded with hard-boiled egg.

Salt beef Prepared the same way as corned beef but with brisket.

Schmaltz Chicken fat which has been rendered down with onion.

Tzimmes A side dish of sweetened vegetables and fruits, usually carrot and apple.

KOREAN

Bap/babe Rice.

Ben jang au Small filleted Korean eels, braised in soy sauce, sesame oil, sugar, garlic and chilli.

Bi bim bap Rice, vegetables and meat served on a Japanese-style hot stone, often with a raw or fried egg on top.

Bintatok/bindaeduk Mashed green beans shaped into a pizza-like pancake, usually topped with meat, seafood or vegetables.

Bugalbee Marinated and barbecued beef spare ribs.

Bulgogi/bul-ko-kee Slices of marinated beef barbecued at the table and often served rolled in a lettuce leaf and eaten with vegetable relishes.

Chap chee/jap chee Noodles or transparent vermicelli cooked with beef and mixed vegetables.

Gim/kee Dried seaweed toasted and seasoned with salt and sesame oil.

Gu shul pan A traditional lacquered tray with nine compartments containing different appetisers.

Hobak chun/hobak jun Sliced marrow fried in a light egg batter.

Junglang Rice wine or sake.

Kim chee/kimchi Chinese cabbage, white radishes, cucumber or greens pickled and served with a spicy chilli sauce.

Kook/gook/kuk The name given to any soup, varying from a consommé-like liquid to heavy meaty broths containing noodles, dumplings, meat or fish.

Ko sari na mool/gosari namul Cooked bracken stalks dressed with sesame seeds.

Na mool/namul Vegetable side dishes.

Man doo kook Clear soup with steamed meat dumplings.

Pahb Rice

Shinsonro/shinsuiro/sin sollo Known as the 'royal casserole', this meat soup with seaweed, seafood, eggs and vegetables is cooked at the table.

So-joo Strong Korean rice wine drunk as an aperitif.

Yuk hwe Shredded raw beef, strips of pear and egg yolk served chilled.

MALAYSIAN AND INDONESIAN

Archar Assorted pickled vegetables, which may include carrots, beans and onions, spiced with turmeric and pepper.

Assam Tamarind.

Ayam Chicken.

Blachan Dried fermented shrimp paste. It has an unpleasant smell when raw, but adds a piquant fishy taste to cooked dishes.

Char kway teow Stir-fry of wide white rice flour noodles with vegetables and/or meat.

Chendol A dessert containing noodles made from green peas and coloured with green food colouring which is served cold with palm sugar and coconut milk.

Daging Beef.

Gado gado A salad of blanched vegetables topped with a peanut sauce.

Goreng Anything fried in a wok!

Gula melaka Palm sugar.

Ikan Fish.

Kari Curry.

Kambing Lamb.

Kerupuk Similar to prawn crackers.

Kueh A general term for many desserts.

Laksa Originally from Singapore, this noodle soup is made with prawns, chicken, beansprouts, fishcakes and chillies with a coconut cream base.

Kelapa Coconut.

Mee goreng Meat, vegetables or prawns fried with egg noodles.

Mee hoon Rice vermicelli noodles.

Murtabak An Indian/Malaysian pancake of cassava fried on a griddle with a sweet or savoury filling.

Nasi lemak A selection of curries and fish dishes served with a plate of plain boiled rice.

Nasi goreng Fried rice containing shrimp paste, garlic, onions, chillies and soy sauce.

Pergedel A spiced potato cake.

Pisang goreng Banana fritters.

Rempah Generic term used for the fresh curry pastes used in Malaysian cookery.

Rijsttafel An Indonesian set meal of several courses.

Rendang A 'dry curry' containing meat cooked in coconut milk.

Roojak Javanese dish of vegetables and fruit in a spicy sauce.

Roti canai A Southern Indian/Malaysian breakfast dish of round, deep-fried bread served with either a small dish of chicken curry or dhal.

Sambal There are several types of sambal, often made from hot chilli sauce, onions and coconut oil, and either used as a side dish or to flavour main dishes.

Satay Skewered chicken, beef, prawns or fish, barbecued and served with a sauce of ground peanuts, chilli, onions and sugar.

Sayur Vegetables.

Soto Soup.

Sotong Squid.

Tahu Tofu.

Telor Egg.

Tempeh An Indonesian fermented soy bean product similar to tofu, but with a more varied texture. It can even resemble peanut butter in appearance.

Udang Prawns or shrimps.

Albondigas Meat balls containing olives, chilli powder, eggs, spices, herbs, onions and bread which are simmered in stock with garlic and tomatoes.

Bunuelos Light biscuit fritters sprinkled with icing sugar and cinnamon and eaten freshly fried with coffee.

Burritos A dish made from rolled pancakes filled with chilli con carne and coated with cheese sauce, accompanied by salad and extra grated cheese.

Cabrito asado Roast baby kid flavoured with garlic and chilli powder.

Ceviche Raw white fish cut into cubes and marinated in lime juice, lemon juice, garlic, onions, chillies and seasonings.

Chiles rellenos A speciality made from strips of corn tortilla which are fried until crisp, reheated with tomato sauce and garnished with grated cheese, chopped chillies and onions.

Chille con carne A dish of stewed meat, simmered with onions, garlic, tomatoes, chilli powder, red kidney beans, spices and sometimes extra chilli. It is a served with refried beans, tortillas, white rice and salad.

Chimichangas Fried stuffed tacos made from flour tortillas which puff up when fried. Traditionally filled with a minced beef mixture and accompanied by shredded lettuce, grated cheese, sliced radishes and chopped spring onions.

Corn chips See *tortilla chips*.

Empanadas Pastry turnovers containing sweet or savoury fillings which are either baked or shallow-fried.

Frijoles refritos This dish of refried beans consists of either red kidney, pinto, pink or black beans boiled until tender with onions, garlic, chillies and tomatoes and served with tortillas.

Guacamole Made from avocados, lemon or lime juice, onion, tomatoes, green chillies, coriander and seasonings all mashed together and served either as a dip or an accompaniment to many dishes.

Masa harina This particular type of cornflour is treated with lime water and used to make tortillas.

Mole A sauce made from chillies, onion, garlic, tomatoes, spices, tortillas which thicken, raisins which sweeten and chocolate which darkens.

Mole poblana de guajalote The national dish of Mexico made with turkey and mole sauce.

Nachos Made from pieces of fried tortilla, these are often served topped with cheese and grilled and garnished with green chilli.

Picadillo Minced pork, beef, onions, oil, tomato, garlic, vinegar, raisins, chopped almonds, spices, herbs and seasonings used as a filling or served with rice as a main course.

Quesadillas Tortillas sandwiched together with cheese, onions and chillies and served hot.

Sopa de aguacate Avocado soup.

Taco shells Fried tortilla shells filled with salad, chilli con carne, guacamole and refried beans.

Tacos The Mexican term for small tortillas.

Tostados Medium-sized tortillas fried until crisp and topped with meat, poultry, fish or cheese and seasoned with chilli sauce.

Totopos Tortilla chips.

Baba ganoush Egyptian name for a purée of toasted aubergines mixed with sesame sauce, garlic and lemon juice.

Baklava Filo pastry layered up with pistachio nuts, almonds and walnuts and then soaked in syrup.

Basturma Smoked beef.

Briwats Similar to spring rolls filled with vegetables.

Blintzes Heavy vegetable pancakes filled with savoury mash or cheese.

Burghul Cracked wheat.

Falafel/felafel A mixture of spicy ground chick-peas or broad beans rolled into balls and served with houmous or tahini.

Fatayer A soft pastry with fillings of cheese, onions, spinach and pine kernels.

Fatoush Lebanese bread, toasted and filled with fresh vegetables.

Fu'l Brown broad beans seasoned with olive oil, lemon juice, garlic and sprinkled with parsley, and often served with hard-boiled eggs.

Houmous Ground chick-peas blended with oil, garlic, tahini and lemon juice to make a creamy paste.

Kibbeh Minced lamb, crushed wheat, and onions are mixed together and formed into balls which are deep-fried. The mixture can also be served raw as *kibbeh nayeh* accompanied by lettuce.

Kofta Minced lamb or beef combined with eggs, onions and spices, shaped into a sausage-like shape and barbecued.

Konafa Cake made from shredded pastry dough and filled with syrup and nuts or cream.

Kubbe Minced lamb or beef mixed with burghul, then deep fried.

Labneh Middle Eastern version of cream cheese.

Lahmi meshwi/shish kebab Cubes of marinated meat grilled on a skewer, it can also include onions, pepper and tomatoes, served either in pitta bread or with rice.

Ma'amoul Different shaped pastries filled with nuts or dates.

Maklubi Upside down cake of rice, lamb, aubergine and other vegetables.

Molokhia A soupy stew made with molokhia leaves and meat.

Moutabel Middle Eastern name for purée of toasted aubergines mixed with sesame sauce, garlic and lemon.

Muhallabia A milky pudding made from ground rice with the addition of almonds and pistachios, and flavoured with rose-water or orange blossom.

Om ali Bread-and-butter pudding made with raisins.

Sambousek Small pastries filled with mince, onion and pine kernels.

Tabouleh A salad of crushed wheat, chopped parsley, tomatoes, onion, olive oil and lemon juice.

Tahina Thin paste made from sesame seeds.

Shashlik Marinated meat and vegetables on a skewer.

Shawarma Slices of marinated lamb grilled on a spit and sliced kebab style.

Shish taouk Grilled cubes of chicken served with a lemon and garlic sauce.

Tagine A traditional Moroccan cooking pot consisting of a base, and a tepee-shaped lid with a small hole in the top to allow the steam to escape. Vegetables, meat and fish are cooked in stews in the oven and served in the dish.

Tahini Sesame seed sauce.

Tamaya Egyptian name for falafel.

Warak einab Stuffed vine leaves.

Alpino Salami.

Anchovy paste Anchovy essence.

Arugula Rocket.

Bacon Canadian gammon steak.

Baking soda Bicarbonate of soda.

Barley Pearl barley.

Beans, bush Dwarf beans.

Beans, garbanzo Chick-peas.

Beans, Boston Haricot beans.

Beans, string French beans.

Beets Beetroot.

Biscuit Scone.

Broil Grill.

Broiler, chicken Spring chicken/poussin.

Butter, drawn Clarified butter.

Butter, sweet Unsalted butter.

Whipped butter Margarine.

Candy Sweets.

Candy, cotton Candy floss.

Catsup Tomato ketchup.

Celery root Celeriac.

Cheese, American Processed cheese/Kraft singles.

Charqui Sun-dried strips of beef or venison.

Chicory Endive.

Cilantro Coriander.

Collard greens Spring greens/curly kale.

Corned beef Salt beef.

Cornmeal Polenta.

Cornstarch Cornflour.

Corn syrup Golden syrup.

Cotto Salami made from pork and peppercorns.

Cream, heavy Whipping cream or double cream.

Cream, light Single cream.

Cymling squash or patty pan Spaghetti squash.

Dutch oven Flameproof casserole.

Eggplant Aubergine.

Egg roll Spring roll.

Fish sticks Fish fingers.

Flan Creme caramel.

Flounder Plaice.

Flour, all purpose Plain flour.

Flour, bread Strong flour.

Frank Frankfurter.

Frosting Icing.

Green onions Spring onions or salad onions.

Grinder Baguette with filling.

Hard sauce Brandy or rum butter.

Head cheese Brawn.

Indian corn Maize.

Indian rice Wild rice.

Jello Jelly.

Jelly roll Swiss roll.

Jicama White radish.

Kasha Roasted buckwheat.

Legumes Pulses.

Lettuce, romaine Cos lettuce.

Lox Smoked salmon.

Manicotti Cappelletti.

Masa harina Coarse cornmeal.

Mimosa Buck's fizz.

Mush A type of porridge made from cornmeal.

Oleo Margarine.

Pan-broil Dry frying.

Papaya Paw paw.

Peppers, bell Sweet peppers.

Planked Term for food cooked or served on a plank.

Rutabaga Swede (or turnip in Scotland).

Scallions Spring or salad onions.

Skillet Frying pan.

Snow peas Mange tout.

Squab A small one portion chicken or a four-week old pigeon.

Sugar, confectioner's Icing sugar.

Sugar, superfine Caster sugar.

Sugar, turbinado Demerara sugar.

Tangelo A cross between a grapefruit and an orange.

Tomato paste Double concentrated tomato purée.

Tomato Purée Creamed tomatoes or puréed tinned tomatoes.

Turnip, French White-fleshed swedes.

Vanilla bean Vanilla pod.

Variety meats Offal.

Zucchini Courgettes.

SCANDINAVIAN

D = Danish   F = Finnish
N = Norwegian   S = Swedish

Aeblekage D A dessert made from apple purée layered up with breadcrumbs fried in butter with sugar.

Aebleskiver D A kind of non-yeasted doughnut with an apple filling cooked in a special cast iron pan with seven indentations.

Aeggekage D Similar to an omelette, this Danish egg cake is left unfolded and topped with bacon rashers.

Ärter med fläsk S Split pea and pork soup served traditionally every Thursday in winter.

Biff à la Lindstom S Raw minced beef, mashed potatoes, cream, chopped beetroot, onion, capers and seasoning are made into cakes and fried with onions.

Bløtkake N A layered sponge cake with cream which is sometimes coated in marzipan.

Bondepige med slør D Similar to aeblekage, but crumbled rye bread is used instead of regular breadcrumbs and melted red jam is added to the apple purée. A national favourite.

Bruna bönor S Soaked brown beans are simmered in water until soft, then salt, vinegar and sugar are added and it is served with pork dishes.

Brunede kartofler D New potatoes fried in butter and sugar until golden.

Danish Pastry D A yeasted puff pastry is used to make these delicious Danish speciality pastries.

Dansk leverpostej D Danish liver pate made from calf's liver, flour, cream, egg, onion, butter and seasonings. It is either served warm with new potatoes or used to top sandwiches.

Danska wienerbrød D Danish pastries shaped into pinwheels, crescents, stars and cockscombs.

Får i kål N A lamb and cabbage stew served with boiled potatoes.

Ferske reker N Fresh shrimp.

Fiskboller N Cod or haddock fish balls, poached in fish stock and served with either a white or cheese sauce.

Fiskesuppe N Fish soup.

Fløtekarameller N Caramel cream, a firm favourite with the Norwegians.

Frikadeller D Pork or beef meatballs which are fried until golden brown and then served with potatoes and red cabbage or salad.

Glasmästarsill S Herrings which have been marinated in vinegår and sugar over two days, then placed in a glass jar and stored in the refrigerator, also known as glass blower's herring.

Gravlax S Marinated or sugar-cured salmon made from raw fish.

Grystek S Pot-roasted beef or reindeer

served with boiled potatoes, vegetables and redcurrant jelly.

Gule aerter D A winter soup made from yellow split peas, mixed vegetables and belly of pork.

Hasselback potatoes S Peeled medium-sized potatoes are scored downwards into thin slices without cutting right through, brushed with butter and baked in the oven. Half way through cooking they are sprinkled with cheese.

Inlagd gurka S A sweet and sour cucumber salad garnished with chopped parsley or dill.

Inlagd sill S Pickled herring, traditionally served with boiled potatoes or bread and butter.

Jansson's temptation S A dish made from grated or julienned raw potatoes, chopped onions, butter, anchovy, cream and breadcrumbs.

Julefrokest D The name given to the Danish Christmas cold table, featuring a whole cooked Danish gammon.

Juleskinka S Ham served hot or cold at Christmas with the words 'God Jul' piped on top.

Kalakeitto F A soup made from milk, lake fish, onions, rye bread and potatoes, thickened with cornflour and garnished with chopped dill.

Kalakukko F Hollowed-out rye loaf filled with fish, similar to whitebait, and fat pork. This is then baked slowly in the oven.

Käldolmar S Cabbage rolls stuffed with minced beef, rice, milk and water, lightly fried and coated with a syrup, baked in stock and served with boiled potatoes and cranberry sauce.

Kokt torsk S Poached cod served with melted butter or hot white sauce to which chopped hard-boiled eggs have been added, served with boiled potatoes.

Koldebord D Danish equivalent of Smörgåsbord.

Koldtbord N Norway's version of the open table.

Karelian open pasties F These look like flat elongated ovals made from rye dough and filled with a cooked rice mixture. They are served warm and topped with a mixture of chopped hard-boiled eggs and butter.

Karjalanpaisti F A casserole made from diced beef, pork, lamb and vegetables, served with boiled potatoes and mashed swedes.

Köttbullar S Minced beef meat balls served with creamed potatoes and cranberry sauce.

Kumpe N Potato flour dumpling.

Lefse N Light unsweetened griddle cake.

Lohikeitto F Salmon soup containing leeks and potatoes.

Lohipiiras F Salmon pie similar to the Russian koulibiac.

Lumpe N Potato flour pancake.

Lutefisk N Dried cod.

Maksalaatikko F A liver pudding made from rice, milk, water, onion, liver, syrup, raisins, eggs and marjoram, served with boiled potatoes and cranberry sauce.

Patakukko F A double-crusted pie made from rye dough and filled with little fish, similar to whitebait, called muikko and fat pork.

Pepparkaakor S Biscuits spiced with cinnamon, cloves and ground cardamom and traditionally served at Christmas.

Plättar S Pancakes which are rolled up and served with jam, traditionally served after pea and pork soup on winter Thursdays.

Pytt i panna S Fried potato cubes, onions, cubed ham and beef served with a raw egg stirred into the hash.

Reker N Boiled shrimp.

Risengrød D A rice soup or porridge served at Christmas before the main course, sprinkled with sugar and cinnamon and topped off with knobs of butter. The person who finds the hidden whole almond is rewarded with a gift of marzipan.

Saffraansbørd S This saffron yeasted fruit bread is traditionally served on the thirteenth of December, the festival of Santa Lucia.

Sandkage D Similar to Madeira cake, but made with a mixture of flour and cornflour or potato flour.

Semlor S Served in bowls of hot milk, these spicy, yeasted buns are made for Shrove Tuesday.

Silde N Herring.

Smörgåsbord S The famous open table might include a variety of herring dishes, three or four egg dishes, fifteen to twenty hot and cold meat and poultry dishes, nine or ten condiments or salads, an assortment of crispbreads, bread and cheese, fruit and desserts. It is thought impolite to pile your plate up, but best to return for each course for a clean plate.

Smørrebrød D There are over six hundred different variations of this famous Danish open sandwich.

Spekemat N Wind-dried meat.

Swedish anchovies S Sprat, canned in oil.

Torsketungur N Cod tongues.

Varm polse N Hot dogs.

Västkustsallad S A salad made from prawns, lobster, mussels, peas, mushrooms, tomato and asparagus flavoured with dill and garnished with mayonnaise and dill.

Vispi puuro F The sweetened juice from summer berries is cooked with semolina, then beaten off the heat until very light and frothy, and served with sprinkled sugar and milk.

SPANISH

Aceitunas Olives.

All-i-oli Catalan olive oil and garlic sauce.

Bacalao Dried and salted cod.

Bonito Tuna.

Bullabesa A fish soup, similar to the French bouillabaisse.

Calamares Squid.

Chorizo A salami type sausage made from pork, pieces of fat, garlic and paprika, hence the orange colour. Served as an appetiser or as a main course with chick-peas.

Churros Fritters sprinkled with sugar and eaten for breakfast.

Cocido a la madrilena A slow-cooked stew made from meat, fowl, vegetables, sausage and chick-peas.

Crema catalana Spanish-style crème brûlée.

Ensalada de arroz Rice salad.

Escabeche de conejo Marinated rabbit.

Gambas Prawns.

Gazpacho A chilled soup from Andalucia made from a purée of tomato, red pepper, garlic, onion, oil, vinegar, water, seasoning and breadcrumbs, often served with dishes of croutons, diced cucumber, diced green pepper and chopped onion.

Gypsy's arm A Swiss roll filled with jam or strawberries and cream.

Jamon serrano The best of the Spanish hams.

Manchego A hard cheese made from ewe's milk from La Mancha.

Olla porida A rich, highly seasoned stew.

Paella A savoury mixture of rice, vegetables, chicken and shellfish to which saffron is added.

Pollo a la chilindron Chicken with peppers, tomatoes and olives.

Romesco sauce A Catalan sauce made from hot red romesco peppers, garlic, blanched almonds, tomato, olive oil and red wine vinegar.

Tapas These highly spiced little snacks are served in advance of or instead of a main meal and can consist of virtually anything. Meatballs, fried aubergine, anchovies, vegetable salads, tortilla, prawns in garlic, etc. can be found in bars at any time of day.

Tortilla An omelette containing fried potato and onion. Sometimes sweet red pepper and chopped tomato are added.

Zarzuela A shellfish and seafood stew.

THAI

Bai horapa/bai horopa Thai basil or holy basil, darker than European basil and with an aniseed flavour.

Ba mi Egg noodles.

Galangal Similar to common ginger, used fresh.

Gaeng Curry. Yellow is the mildest, followed by red and green which are medium-hot.

Hoi Shellfish.

Kaeng chud woon sen Clear noodle soup with minced pork or chicken.

Kai Chicken.

Kecap Similar to soy sauce but sweeter and thicker.

Khanom A starter of dim sum.

Khantoke A North Eastern banquet conducted around a low table while seated on triangular cushions.

Khanom pang na koong Prawn sesame toast.

Khao/kow Rice.

Khao nao North Eastern sticky rice.

Khao pat Fried rice.

Khao suay/na Steamed rice.

Khing With ginger.

Kung Prawns.

Kratiem Garlic.

Kratong thong Tiny crispy batter cups filled with mixed vegetables and/or minced meat.

Kwaitiew Noodles.

Larb A salad of minced and cooked meat with lime juice, ground rice and herbs.

Ma-grood Kaffir lime. The leaves are used in cooking and have a citrus flavour.

Makua paw/ma-khhue puang A baby green aubergine.

Maprao Coconut.

Mee krob Sweet, crispy fried vermicelli.

Mu Pork.

Nam pla Fish sauce, commonly used as a condiment in Thailand.

Nam prik A hot sauce made from red chillies and fermented shrimp paste.

Nua Beef.

Op/ob Baked.

Pad/pat Stir-fried.

Pad si-ewe Noodles fried with mixed meat in soya sauce.

Pad Thai Stir-fried noodles with shrimps, chicken or pork, beansprouts, salted turnips and ground peanuts.

Pak chee Coriander.

Palm sugar A dark brown sugar made from the sap of oriental palm trees.

Pandan leaf Malaysian screwpine leaf used in cooking.

Papaya An unripened papaya.

Pat khai Egg-fried rice.

Pea aubergines These are expensive and very slightly bitter and English peas may be used as a substitute.

Pet/pepoh tak Hot and sour mixed seafood soup.

Pla Fish.

Pla meuk Squid.

Porpia Spring rolls.

Prik Chillies.

Sen mei Rice vermicelli.

Sen lek Medium size flat noodle, used to make pad Thai.

Sen yai Wide flat rice noodles.

Som tam A popular cold salad of grated green papaya.

Ta-krai Lemongrass or citronella. They look like small leeks, are tough and inedible, but give a wonderful citrus flavour in Thai cooking.

Tod Deep-fried.

Tod mun pla Small fried fish cakes.

Tom Boiled.

Tom kha kai Hot and sour chicken soup with coconut milk.

Tom yam A watery hot and sour soup made with lemongrass, mushroom, and prawns.

Tom yam kai Soup with chicken.

Tom yam hed Soup with mushrooms.

Yang Barbecued or roasted.

Woon sen Transparent vermicelli made from soybeans or other pulses.

Yam/yum A hot and sour tossed salad flavoured with lemon and chilli.

Yam nua Hot and sour beef salad.

Yam talay Hot and sour seafood salad.

Zerumbet/krachai Smaller than galangal but with a milder taste.

TURKISH

Ayran A drink similar to the Indian lassi.

Bamye A stew made from minced lamb, okra, tomato, onion, lemon and green pepper.

Beyendi Aubergine purée made from a white sauce, sometimes including Swiss cheese.

Biber dolmasi Sweet peppers stuffed with onions, raisins, pinenuts and rice, baked in the oven and served lightly chilled.

Borek Spinach, meat or cheese pastries, made with filo pastry. The most common ones are muska and peynirli boreks.

Cay Strong black tea served in glasses and heavily sweetened.

Comlek kebabi A lamb and mixed vegetable stew served with boiled potatoes or pilav.

Dolma Stuffed vegetables.

Domates dolmasi Tomatoes stuffed with onions, raisins, pine nuts and rice, baked in the oven and served slightly chilled.

Doner kebapi/doner kebab A huge layered lamb kebab which is cooked upright on a skewer turning over an intense heat source.

Fasulya plaki A haricot bean salad including onions, oil, tomato and red or green pepper.

Fava A broad bean paste, similar to houmous.

Houmous A creamy paste made from chick peas, tahini, garlic, oil & lemon juice.

Ic pilav A pilav made from round-grain rice, fried onions, pine nuts, chopped lamb's liver, currants, tomato, cinnamon and stock.

Iskender kebab A combination of doner with tomato sauce, yoghurt and melted butter on bread.

Kabac dolmasi Young marrows or courgettes stuffed with onions, raisins, rice and pinenuts, baked in the oven and served slightly chilled.

Kabak tathsi A dessert made from cooked pumpkin soaked in syrup and sprinkled with walnuts.

Kadin gobegi Small fried biscuits.

Khave Strong black coffee.

Kisir A mixture of chopped parsley,

tomatoes, onions, crushed wheat, olive oil and lemon juice.

Kofte Fried meat balls made from beef.

Lokum Turkish delight.

Manca Spinach and yoghurt with garlic.

Manti Fresh ravioli coated with a yoghurt sauce.

Mezeter An assortment of different dishes served as an appetiser.

Musakka Layers of fried aubergine, onions, minced lamb or beef, tomatoes and green peppers.

Pide Pitta bread.

Pilaki Fish cutlets simmered with vegetables and garlic, served cold with lemon and parsley. It is also the name for beans in olive oil.

Pilav Round grain rice cooked until soft with the addition of butter.

Raki A strong aniseed-flavoured drink.

Shashk Rolled lamb on a skewer.

Sis kebab The national dish of Turkey, this consists of skewered cubed lamb cooked under a grill and served with grilled peppers and tomatoes and pilav.

Sis kofte Skewered lamb meatballs grilled and served with pilav.

Sucuk Sliced spicy sausage.

Suttac Rice pudding served with ice cream.

Turlu Mixed vegetable stew.

Yogurtlu Minced lamb on a bed of bread and yoghurt.

Zeytinyagli sebzeter A speciality mixed vegetable stew served slightly chilled.

Appendices

Weights and measures

International conversion tables

Measure	UK	Australia	USA
1 pint	20 fl oz	20 fl oz	20 fl oz
1 cup	10 fl oz	8 fl oz	8 fl oz
1 tablespoon	5/8 fl oz	1/2 fl oz	1/2 fl oz
1 dessertspoon	2/5 fl oz	no official measure	
1 teaspoon	1/5 fl oz	1/8 fl oz	1/6 fl oz

NB All spoon measurements are based on a level spoonful unless otherwise stated.

In British cookery books a gill is 5 fl oz / 1/4 pt
Other approximate non-standardised measures include
Breakfast cup 10 fl oz
Tea cup 5 fl oz
Coffee cup 3 fl oz
1 tablespoon 3 teaspoons
1 level tablespoon 15 ml
1 level dessertspoon 10 ml
1 level teaspoon   5 ml

The following ingredients measured in level tablespoons weigh approximately 1 oz

Tablespoons to 1 oz	Ingredient
1	salt syrup honey treacle jam
2	dried nuts rice
3	breadcrumbs (dry) demerara sugar icing sugar semolina flour cornflower custard powder
4	porridge oats ground almonds hazelnuts walnuts cocoa powder
5	grated cheese dessicated coconut
6	breadcrumbs (fresh)

Imperial weight for various ingredients and the American equivalent in cups and tablespoons

Imperial	Ingredient	American
1 lb	butter or fat	2 cups
1 lb	flour	4 cups
1 lb	granulated or castor sugar	2 cups
1 lb	icing sugar or confectioner's sugar	3 cups
1 lb	brown sugar	2 2/3 cups
1 lb	syrup or treacle	1 cup
1 lb	rice	2 cups
1 lb	dried fruit	2 cups
1 lb	chopped meat	2 cups
1 lb	lentils or split peas	2 cups
1 lb	fresh breadcrumbs	4 cups
1/2 oz	flour	1 level tablespoon
1 oz	flour	1 heaped tablespoon
1 oz	sugar	1 level tablespoon
1/2 oz	butter	1 level tablespoon

Conversions from Imperial to metric and metric to Imperial

NB Recipes will usually round down for conversions from Imperial to metric, eg. 1oz is often taken as equivalent to 25g, but sometimes 1oz will be rounded up to 30g. The following conversion tables do not round up or down to whole numbers so that a true picture of the equivalents can be seen. Figures are taken from the British Standards tables.

Capacity

Imperial to metric (fluid ounces/pints to millilitres)

fl oz (fluid ounce)	pt (pint)	ml (millilitre)
1 fl oz		28.41 ml
5 fl oz	1/4 pt (1 gill)	142.06 ml
10 fl oz	1/2 pt	284.12 ml
15 fl oz	3/4 pt	426.18 ml
20 fl oz	1 pt	568.24 ml
40 fl oz	2 pt (1 quart/1 qt)	1136.49 ml (1.14l)
160 fl oz	8 pt (1 UK gallon/1 gal)	4545.96 ml (4.55l)

NB Most recipe books give 20 fl oz (1pint) as equivalent to 600 ml (actual 568.24 ml)

Metric to Imperial (millilitres to fluid ounces)

ml (millilitre)	fl oz (fluid ounce)
1 ml	0.03520 fl oz
5 ml	0.17598 fl oz
10 ml	0.35196 fl oz
15 ml	0.52794 fl oz
20 ml	0.70392 fl oz
50 ml	1.75980 fl oz
100 ml	3.51961 fl oz
250 ml	8.79903 fl oz
500 ml	17.59805 fl oz
1000 ml (1 litre/1l)	35.19610 fl oz

Weight

Imperial to metric (ounces/pounds to grams)

oz (ounce)	lb (pound)	g (gram)
1 oz		28.350 g
2 oz		56.699 g
4 oz	1/4 lb	113.398 g
8 oz	1/2 lb	226.796 g
12 oz	3/4 lb	340.194 g
16 oz	1 lb	453.592 g
32 oz	2 lb	907.184 g

NB Most recipe books give 1 oz as equivalent to 25 g (actual 28.35 g)

Metric to Imperial (grams to ounces)

g (gram)	oz (ounce)
10 g	0.35274 oz
20 g	0.70548 oz
50 g	1.76370 oz
100 g	3.52740 oz
125 g	4.40925 oz
150 g	5.29109 oz
175 g	6.17294 oz
200 g	7.05479 oz
225 g	7.93664 oz
250 g	8.81849 oz
500 g	17.6370 oz
1000 g (1 kilogram/1kg)	35.2736 oz

Oven temperatures

In this table the Gas Mark is given and the standard Fahrenheit temperature. Most tables give a rounded up or down equivalent Celsius (Centigrade) temperature. This table gives the true equivalent to one decimal place and then the value rounded up or down to the nearest 5°.

Gas mark	Description	°F (Fahrenheit)	°C Celsius (actual)	°C (to 5°)
1/4	very cool	225	107.2	105
1/2	very cool	250	121.1	120
1	cool	275	135.0	135
2	cool	300	148.9	150
3	very moderate	325	162.8	165
4	moderate	350	176.7	175
5	moderately hot	375	190.6	190
6	moderately hot	400	204.4	205
7	hot	425	218.3	220
8	hot	450	232.2	230
9	very hot	475	246.1	245

It should be noted that these temperatures are only an approximate guide as all ovens vary slightly according to the make and country of origin.

Index

Beech 80
Beef 22
Beet greens 58
Beetroot 49
Belgian endive 58
Bergamot 83
Berry fruits 66
Betel 80
Beurre blanc 135
Beurre composé 135
Beurre manie 3
Bicarbonate of soda 3
Bigarade 135
Bilberry 66
Binding 106
Bio yoghurt 42
Biscuit 3
Biscuit cutters 98
Bitter almond 80
Bitter orange 68
Black bean 63
Black bread 120
Black butter sauce 135
Black fermented
    Chinese bean 63
Black mullet 32
Black mustard seed 87
Black peppercorn 87
Black peppercorn 89
Black salsify 49
Black treacle 147
Blackberry 66
Blackcurrant 66
Black-eyed bean 63
Blanching 106
Blancmange 3
Blanquette 3
Blender 92
Blending 106
Blewitt 61
Blood orange 68
Bloomer loaf 120

Blow torch 92
Blue crab 35
Blue fish 31
Blue pea 63
Blueberry 66
Bluefin tuna 34
Boar 28
Boat mould 92
Boiling 106
Boiling fowl 25
Boletus 61
Bolognaise sauce 135
Boning 106
Boning knife 96
Bonito 31
Borage 83
Bordelaise sauce 135
Borlotto bean 63
Boston 58
Boston bean 63
Boston bluefish 31
Boston brown
    bread 120
Bottling 106
Bouchée 3
Bounceberry 66
Bouquet garni 3
Boysenberry 66
Bozzoli 128
Braising 106
Bramble 66
Bran 43
Brassicas 57
Brazil 80
Bread 4
Bread knife 96
Bread sauce 135
Breadfruit 53
Bridge roll 120
Brill 31
Brining 107
Brioche 121

Brisling 34
Broad bean 56
Broad bean 63
Broccoli 57
Brochette 4
Broiling 107
Brown rice 46
Brown sauce 135
Browning 107
Brûlée 4
Brunoise 4
Brussels sprouts 57
Bucatini 127
Buckwheat 44
Buckwheat flour 44
Bulb roaster 92
Bulbs 55
Bulgar wheat 47
Bulghur wheat 47
Bulgur wheat 47
Bun 4
Burbot 29
Burger 4
Burnet 83
Butter 39
Butter 4
Butter bean 64
Butter clam 35
Butterhead 59
Buttermilk 41
Butternut 54
Butternut 80
Butterscoth 4
Button 61

C

Cabbage 57
Caboul sauce 135
Cake 4
Calamondin 68
Callaloo 58
Calves' brains 24

Gurnard 32
Gutting 111

H

Hachinette 96
Haddock 32
Hairy lychee 71
Hake 32
Half cream 41
Half fat butter 39
Halibut 32
Ham 23
Hamburg parsley 50
Hanging 111
Hard sauce 137
Hard-boiling 111
Hare 28
Haricot bean 64
Harissa sauce 137
Harvey sauce 137
Hashing 112
Hawthorn 67
Hazel hen 27
Hazelnut 81
Hazelnut oil 150
Heads 24
Heart of palm 59
Hearts 24
Heating through 112
Hen 27
Herb 10
Herbs 83
Herring 33
Hog plum 71
Hoisin sauce 137
Hollandaise sauce 137
Homogenised milk 42
Honey 148
Honeydew melon 75
Hop 84
Horn of plenty 62
Hors d'oeuvre 10

Horse mushroom 62
Horseradish 50
Horseradish 88
Horseradish relish 144
Horseradish sauce 138
Hot cross bun 122
Hot-water crust 131
Huckleberry 67
Hulling 112
Hungerian sauce 138
Hyssop 84

I

Ice cream 10
Iceberg 59
Icing 10
Icing bag 95
Icing sugar 146
Indian 81
Indonesian relish 144
Infusing 112
Irish soda bread 124
Italian rice 46

J

Jackfish 30
Jackfruit 53
Jaggery 147
Jam 144
Jam sugar 146
Japanese pickled
    relish 144
Jardinière 10
Jelly 145
Jelly bag 95
Jelly mould 95
Jerusalem srtichoke 50
John Dory 33
Johnny cake 122
Jugging 112
Juice extractor 95
Julienne 10

Jumbo oats 45
Juneberry 67
Juniper 89
Junket 10
Jus 10
Jus lié 10

K

Kale 57
Kebab 10
Kecap manis 138
Kemiri 81
Kernel 81
Ketchup 138
Kibbled wheat 48
Kidneys 24
King crab 36
King prawn 36
Kingfish 33
Kitchen scissors 95
Kiwi fruit 71
Kneading 112
Knives 95
Knocking back 112
Knocking up 112
Kolrabi 57
Kosher 10
Kumara 50
Kumquat 69

L

Lablab 64
Lacing 112
Lactic acid 10
Ladies' fingers 56
Ladle 97
Lamb 23
Lamb's lettuce 59
Lampuga 32
Lancette 128
Land cress 59
Lard 10

Larding 112
Larding needle 97
Lardy cake 122
Large white bean 64
Lasagna 126
Lasagne 126
Lasagnette 126
Leaven 10
Leaves 58
Leek 55
Legume 11
Lemon 69
Lemon balm 84
Lemon grass 84
Lemon verbena 84
Lentil 64
Lesser weaver 32
Lettuce 59
Liaising 112
Liaison 11
Light rye bread 122
Lights 24
Ligonberry 67
Lime 69
Lime leaves 84
Lime pickle 143
Limpa bread 123
Ling 33
Lingue di passero 128
Linguine 126
Lining 112
Linseed bread 123
Liquidising 112
Liquorice 89
Liver 24
Loach 30
Loaf sugar 146
Loaf tin 97
Lobster 36
Loganberry 67
Lollo biando 59
Lollo rosso 59

Longan 71
Longfin 34
Long-life milk 42
Loquat 71
Lotus root flour 44
Lovage 85
Lukewarm 11
Lumache medie 128
Lump sugar 147
Lungo-vermicelli coupe 125
Lychee 71
Lyonnaise sauce 138

M

Macadamia 81
Macaroni 127
Macaroon 11
Maccheroni 127
Maccheroni alla chitarra 126
Mace 89
Macedoine 11
Macerating 112
Mâche 59
Mackerel 33
Madeleine 97
Magliette 127
Maize 44
Maize 56
Maize flour 44
Malfalda 126
Malt bread 123
Malt vinegar 151
Maltagliati 128
Maltaise sauce 138
Mandarin 69
Mandolin 97
Mange-tout 56
Mango 71
Mango chutney 142
Mango pickle 143

Mangosteen 71
Manicotti 129
Maple syrup 148
Margarine 11
Margherita 126
Marie Rose sauce 138
Marigold 85
Marinade 11
Marinating 112
Marjoram 85
Marmalade 145
Marrow 54
Marrowbone 25
Maruzze 128
Mashing 113
Masking 113
Matzo 123
Mayonnaise 138
Meagre 33
Measuring jug 97
Measuring spoons 97
Meat 11
Meat tenderiser 97
Medallion 11
Medlar 74
Melba sauce 138
Melon baller 97
Melt 25
Meringue 11
Meunière 11
Mezza luna 96
Mezzane 127
Mignon 11
Milk 11
Milk 41
Milk pan 100
Millet 45
Milling 113
Mimosa 11
Mincemeat 11
Mincing 113
Mineola 69

Sauce 15
Sauce spoon 101
Sauce verte 140
Saury 33
Sausage 15
Sauté pan 100
Sautéeing 115
Savarin 124
Savoy cabbage 57
Scalding 115
Scales 101
Scallion 55
Scallop 37
Scalloping 115
Scandinavian
    crispbread 124
Scone 15
Scoring 115
Scorzonera 49
Scrambling 115
Sea bass 34
Sea bream 34
Sea eel 32
Sea kale beet 57
Seafood 15
Seakale 52
Sealing 115
Searing 115
Seasoning 15
Seasoning 116
Seaweed 60
Seed 15
Seeded fruits 74
Seedless grape 75
Seeds 56
Seeds 87
Seething 116
Semi-skimmed milk 42
Semolina 48
Separating 116
Sesame oil 150
Sesame seed 90

Setting 116
Seville orange 69
Shad 34
Shaddock 69
Shallot 55
Shallow-frying 116
Shanghai 82
Sharon fruit 72
Shea 82
Shell 82
Shell mould 97
Shellfish 16
Shelling 116
Sherry vinegar 151
Shiitake 62
Shoot vegetables 51
Short crust 132
Shredding 116
Shrimp 37
Shrimp paste 140
Sieve 102
Sieving 116
Sifter 102
Sifting 116
Silver hake 35
Simmering 116
Singeing 116
Single cream 41
Skate 34
Skewer 102
Skewering 116
Skillet 102
Skimmed milk 42
Skimmer 102
Skimming 116
Skinning 116
Skipper 33
Slaking 116
Sloe 77
Slotted spoon 102
Smelt 34
Smitane sauce 140

Smoking 116
Snipe 27
Snow pea 56
Soaking 116
Soda bread 124
Sodium bicarbonate 16
Sodium chloride 15
Soft brown sugar 147
Soft-boiling 117
Softening 117
Sole 34
Sorbet 16
Sorrel 60
Sorrel 85
Soubise sauce 140
Soufflé 16
Soufflé dish 102
Soup 16
Sour cream 41
Sour dough 124
Sour sop 73
Soured cream 41
Souring 117
Sousing 117
Soy flour 47
Soy sauce 140
Soya bean oil 150
Soybean 65
Spaghetti 125
Spaghetti squash 55
Spaghettini 125
Spanish chestnut 82
Spanish onion 55
Spanish sauce 141
Spatula 102
Spices 16
Spices 87
Spinach 60
Spirale 129
Spirit vinegar 151
Spit 16
Spit-roasting 117

Further reading

The Oxford Companion to Food, Alan Davidson,
Oxford University Press

'On food and Cooking' The Science and love of the Kitchen, Harold McGee,
Simon & Schuster

The Concise Larousse Gastronomique, Auguste Escoffier,
Hamlyn Publishing Group